The Choice Step Into The Light

Omanzo Barrett

DEDICATION

To: My Love, my Queen, my Fiancé, my Joy, my ride and die Joshanna.
I am glad that you are not like most people and skip over the dedication of this book.
By the time you are reading this, she will be my wife Joshanna Barrett. Joshy you made me know what it means to really love again.
  If it wasn't for you, I would have no business to be in New York City on Valentine's day: much less to be on a train, to get inspired to write this book. This is why this book is dedicated to you. Thank you so much for believing in me and having my back at all times.

I Will Forever Love You.

CONTENTS

ACKNOWLEDGMENTS

How do I say danke (thanks in German), to all who have made this book a reality? Without you, this book would not be possible. I will never be able to thank you all enough for the impact you have on my life, in inspiring me to make the choice to write this book.

God, with you all things are possible. Far too often we neglect to include you and give you the utmost thanks for directing our lives. So I am saying thank you for all that you have done in placing people and resources to make this book a reality.

Iota Barrett, my mother: thank you for giving birth to me and guiding me in the many unorthodox lessons you have taught me. Thank you for not sparing the rod and spoiling the child (I am that child of course). Even though you are not physically here with me, you are still my motivation to make you proud. Without you, there would be no line in this book to be read. Thank You, Miss I

Maxine Cunningham, you became my aunt through the relationship with my lovely fiancé Joshanna. You believe in me so much, even when most will quit. For that reason, I say thank you. You were my accountability partner in writing this book, to the point where not a day could go by without I am urged to send you my daily writing. This accountability actually had me writing at your 60th Birthday Celebration (a wrong choice I must admit); which literally almost ended the relationship with your niece and I. As usual there you were my confidant, offering your wisdom and inspiring us to work things out - and not throw away our beautiful relationship. You made the choice to inspire me in completing this book; and any success that is to come from this book, please note that you played a major role in its success. Thank you so much, Auntie.

Eunice Rashford, my mother in law
I could write an epistle in thanking you, but I'll resist the urge.

How can I forget? I met you while you were doing business in Jamaica, by mere chance. Little did I know that after we shared the same breakfast table, I would fall in love with your one and only daughter Joshanna. If it wasn't for that meeting, and you requesting to share that breakfast table with me, there would be no meeting of your wonderful daughter. Which means there would be no reason for me to be on that train in New York City in February 2018, to get the inspiration in writing this book. You always have been our counselor to get us back on track, each time we got derailed. For that, I say thank you, Mums In Law for accepting me as your son in law.

Joshanna, my Love. Thanks for giving me the freedom and the support for pursuing my entrepreneurial mission - even at times when things might not make sense you still believe in me and supported me. Also, a huge thanks for accepting my invitation to spend the rest of our lives together. It was indeed that choice that causes me to be on that train in New York City, to get the inspiration in producing this book - to inspire others to become their best selves. Thank you, my Queen.

Olando Barrett, my twin brother, my next half, my mastermind alliance, my business partner. Thank you for being the best brother anyone can ask for. Anything I needed information about, you are always able to provide or guide me to get the information that is needed. Thank you for introducing me to the network marketing industry, because this is what indirectly placed me on road to personal development. And this played a major role in motivating me to write this book. You even had to put your special touch to this book, in designing the book cover: thank you, bro.

Thandika Thompson, my best friend. You have not only been a great listener but no matter what I requested of you, no matter how challenging it is you always say, " yes I will get it done." And get it done well. Thank you for assisting me in proofreading this book, I truly appreciate you.

Michael Thomas, my editor, "MGT." I met you through the industry of network marketing and I knew we were going to do something great, but I did not know it would be in this book. Thanks a million, MGT in taking the time to review this book and making the many adjustments and correcting the errors, to shape my vision and make it ready to inspire others to make the choice to step into the light. I owe you.

Contributors

If I am to say thanks to all who have helped in making this book a reality, this book would not be ready anytime soon. So I made the choice to include your names as contributors.

Minnette Anderson - Myers, Ronnie Dane Renford, Andre Durrant, Jamar Wright, Carla Nicholson, Tracey Walshy, Ian Miles, Joel Worrell, Natalie Lue-fang, Napolean Hill, Norman Vincent Peale, Jim Rohn, Usain Bolt, Robert Kiyosaki, Johnny Wimbrey, Michael Jex, Wayne Nugent, KD Knight, Ben Carson, Holton Bugs, Clement Stone.
And to everyone who I may have forgotten, please forgive me and Thank You ALL.

1 INSPIRATION

Why are you not where you want to be?
Why do you struggle?
Why do you keep doing the work you do not like,
for the pay you do not want?
Why are you so angry?
Why are you not in the relationship that you desire?
Why? Why? Why?
The answer to all these questions and more, all
comes down to one simple thing. And if you are
ready, you will discover it - in this book.

On the 15th of February 2018, I was struck
by an epiphany. I was heading to my fiancé's house
in Queens, New York on what she called, " the bad
train." Then literally running to catch a bus in the
rain and finally walking to her home. There must
have been thousands of people going to and fro.
People of all creeds, races, stature, and background
floated on the streets, heading to their various

destinations. They all had one thing in common; the dull, joyless and disinterested look blanketing their faces. Wherever these people were heading, it wasn't somewhere they were excited to get to. Just then I felt their pain.

If you were to ask anyone to describe me: there would be an overwhelming comment made by everyone, "he loves to Laugh". I'm a lover of joy and laughter. However, at that moment there was no laughter in me. The only thing that existed in me at that moment was pain and frustration. This led me to ask myself. Why are these people doing this to themselves, especially in the Land of Opportunity?

I am a Jamaican, born and raised. My wife to be, often calls me a "proud third worlder". As I progressed I pondered more and more, do these people know that they have the power to change their circumstances? I wondered, what could be the reason behind them giving up on their dreams and goals - just to continue on the rat race?

It was sometime after 11 p.m. when I got home. As soon as I got in, I had to inoculate my mind against what I'd witnessed. In this case, the antidote was in this case "The Magic of Thinking Big" by David Schwartz, in the form of an audiobook. Shortly after, I went to bed. My body was asleep but my mind was very much awake. I really wanted to help these people, not only those on the train or on the bus, but countless of other individuals across the world and I have finally found it, in this book you are now reading. THE CHOICE - STEP INTO THE LIGHT, I hope it INSPIRES YOU.

2 MY STORY

Let me take you back to where I believe my process of Stepping into the Light all began.

It was the year 1998 and I was a 10 years old Junior School student. In that same year, my father retired from a company he had been working with for over 20 years. The pension he receives biweekly, since that time to this present day of writing, has never exceeded $4000 JMD - equivalent to about 32 USD. Not much to look forward to, after devoting so many years of your life working. On the other hand, my mother was a housewife with 9 children, and to make matters worse, I am a twin.

If you are thinking, that the number one challenge I experienced while growing was lack of money, then you are ABSOLUTELY RIGHT!. Wants were completely neglected in place of the bare necessities. I can recall on many occasions, my mother would send me to the nearest corner store to purchase table salt, not for cooking as you might be thinking but for brushing our teeth. Looking back at

3

it now, life was a real struggle. There was however, one glimmering light in these hard times; my mother: Iota Barrett.

"Iota" is the 9th letter of the Greek alphabet which means, "an extremely small amount". In reality, this was a contradiction of who my mother was. My mother, may her soul rest in peace, was the definition of a magician and a miracle worker. I marvel even today at how she was able to fund my education from Junior School all the way through University. It filled me with a great deal of pride to have been the first in our family to acquire a college degree and also one of five in my community.

It was on that premise, that when I got my first job after completing college; I made it my duty to ensure that my mom was paid first. It was now my time to take care of her, for all the sacrifices she had made for me.

EYE OPENER / REALITY CHECK

In 2014 my mother called and asked if I could assist her with paying for a doctor's visit. Which cost a measly $5,000 JMD - equivalent to about 40 USD. But I could not find it.
The same feeling of being angry, frustrated and upset, that I had experienced on the train from Times Square to Queens was upon me. I asked myself, " how can I be working and I can not come up with the money needed to assist my mother with something as simple as paying for a doctor's visit,

after all the sacrifices that she had made for me to be where I was?"

Obviously what I was doing was not working at all. My life could not be just going to work from 9-5 for 40 years; living hand to mouth, just to cover the bills and then to retire on a pension plan of maximum 40% of my current salary.
If 100% percent of my salary could not do it, how would 40% be sufficient?

THE CHOICE

Right at that very moment, I made the choice to not follow in the footsteps of my father as well as about 95% of the population. So I unsubscribed from that philosophy of the pension plan and job security. Since making that choice, my life has never been the same. It was that choice that I made 4 years ago, why I am able to write this book that you are now reading at this present moment.

The Choice is yours, now you decide what you are going to do with it.

Success Leaves Clues

Emanuel James Rohn, an Entrepreneur, author and world-renowned motivational speaker, more commonly known as Jim Rohn, put forward this simple yet profound statement, " Success Leaves Clues. " It really does leave powerful clues.

Just in case that statement might be too simple for us to understand, let us dive in and look at the choices a few individuals had to make to bring their **dreams and goals** into reality.

> Mark Zuckerberg, in case you are wondering Mark who…; he co-founded the social media platform, which we all interact with in some way or another called Facebook. I can hear some of you saying, I do not use Facebook and that's cool. However, if you have used any of the services of Whatsapp, whether to make free calls, messaging, etc then you are a user of Facebook; because Whatsapp is owned by Facebook.

> Mark in his sophomore year at Harvard University had the choice between completing his degree or following through with a vision to create a social media platform (Facebook). It is quite obvious the choice he made. How many of us would have made the same choice as Mark? The

answer is not many. I can hear people complaining about waking up out of their beds, traveling for hours to work, standing on their feet for the entire day and getting only a half hour break, if they are lucky. However when I respond by saying, " it is a choice you have made to do that. " Their natural reaction is to get upset and angry. They spend more time defending why they do the work they do not like, for the pay they do not want. All I do at those moments is shake my head. I sincerely hope that you who are reading these words are not like them, and you will make the choice to live the life you've always wanted.

The next time you see the KFC logo, and if you are like most people that will be quite often; please be reminded of the choice that Colonel Harland Sanders made. He was an American Businessman, best known for founding the fast-food chicken restaurant Kentucky Fried Chicken. Sanders was born in 1890 in Henryville, Indiana. When he was six years old, his father passed away leaving Sanders to cook and care for his siblings. In seventh grade, he dropped out of school and left home to go work as a farmhand. Already turning into a tough cookie. At 16, he faked his age to enlist in the United States Army. After being honorably discharged a year later, he got hired by the railway as a laborer. However, he got fired for fighting with a coworker. While he worked for the railway, he studied law until he ruined his legal career by getting into another fight. Sanders was forced to move back in with his mom and get a job selling life insurance. And guess what? He got fired for insubordination. But this guy would not give up.

In 1920, he founded a ferry boat company. Later, he tried cashing in his ferry boat business to create a lamp manufacturing company only to find out that another company already sold a better version of his lamp. This poor guy could not catch a break.

It wasn't until age 40 that he began selling chicken dishes in a service station. As he began to advertise his food, an argument with a competitor resulted in a deadly shootout. Four years later, he bought a motel which burned to the ground along with his restaurant. Yet this determined man rebuilt and ran a new motel until World War II forced him to close it down.

Following the war, he tried to franchise his restaurant. His recipe was rejected 1,009 times before anyone accepted it. Sander's "secret recipe" was coined "Kentucky Fried Chicken", and quickly became a hit. However, the booming restaurant was crippled when an interstate opened nearby

so Sanders sold it and pursued his dream of spreading KFC franchises & hiring KFC workers all across the country.
(Taken from *"The Inspiring Life Story of KFC's Colonel Sanders"* by Rachel Denison)

I believe we can all agree that the Colonel was faced with hard choices all through his life. Also, we can agree that even though these were definitely hard choices to be made, he nonetheless made them. So no matter where you are or how challenging you believe your life is; please take courage from the clues the Colonel has left with us, and make the necessary choices to create that legacy that you were placed here on earth to create.

In March 2014, I was about to experience my first flight at the age of 26. While at the airport waiting to board my flight, I had the pleasure of seeing the fastest man alive for the very first time. Unfortunately, he had missed his flight. I am making reference to none other than, The Honorable Usain Saint Leo Bolt. That misfortune allowed me to at least mumble a few words to this superstar and even got to capture a photograph with him.

Before Usain became the legend that he is known to be today or arguably the greatest sprinter of all time, he had to make a series of choices. One of those choices was to either quit after not qualifying for his first Olympics Final, or remain in the sport to become a legend.

The 2004 Games of the XXVIII Olympiad in Athens, Greece was a crossroads for Usain. He was eliminated in the first round of the 200M - due to a leg injury. "At this point, I wanted to quit", were Usain's words in countless interviews. However we know what happened, he made the choice to persevere. He made the choice to stick to his goal of making an impact, not only in athletics but right around the world. Subsequent to that choice, in 2005 he decided to make a fresh start in the form of a new coach; Glen Mills. And as the saying goes, the rest is history.

You do not have to be an aspiring athlete to make use of these clues, neither you have to be an aspiring engineer or a computer programmer. Whatever success means for you; in order to achieve it, you have to choose to press along when faced with obstacles and challenges. So make the choice to remain focus on your dreams and goals, then go further and take the steps to make them a reality.

The Word Impossible

When was the last time you uttered the word IMPOSSIBLE, or any of its derivatives: difficult, unbearable, intolerable, unendurable, unsustainable? Quite often, right?

Well, let us take a look at a story of Sir Roger Gilbert Bannister. Roger Bannister was a British middle-distance athlete, doctor, and academic who ran the first sub-4-minute mile. According to popular beliefs, it was impossible for a man to run a mile in less than 4 minutes. As you would have realized by now *popular beliefs are not necessarily facts*.

On the 6th of May 1954 at Iffley Road Track in Oxford England, the stage was set for about 3,000 spectators to witness this historic event. Before the race, Roger Bannister as you can imagine had to train and prepare his body and mind to accomplish this elusive goal.

In an article entitled, "*Too Modest by Half – Reliving Sir Roger Bannister's Four-Minute Mile*" by the Oxford Royale Academy, this was how the race unfolded. The race started as scheduled 6:00 pm sharp, with Brasher and Bannister immediately taking the lead.

Brasher, wearing No. 44, led both the first lap in 58 seconds and the half-mile in 1:58, with Bannister (No. 41) tucked in behind, and Chataway (No. 42) a stride behind Bannister. Chataway moved to the front after the second lap and maintained the pace with a 3:01 split at the bell. Chataway continued to lead around the front turn until Bannister began his finishing kick with about 275 yards to go (just over a half-lap), running the last lap in just under 59 seconds.

This was very astonishing. However, what is more astonishing is that Bannister's record only lasted for 46 days. What is even more astonishing is, at the present time of writing this book over 1,000 men have run the mile in less than 4 minutes.

So going back to the question which was asked earlier, in regards to when was the last time you used the word impossible or any of its derivatives.

If your answer was quite often. I am suggesting, that you not only take the clues that were laid out above and make the choice to eradicate the word impossible from your vocabulary. But I am also suggesting, that you go forth to create the future of your Dreams.

Your Dreams are Possible, just make the choice.

As humans, it is our natural tendency to take many things for granted. For example, when you step into your home and flip a switch, *flick!!* light appears - more often than not. But have we ever stop and pondered what made it possible for there to be electricity? Apart from saying our bills are paid so we must receive electricity in return, there are a lot more things to consider.

Since the beginning of time, they have been various light sources. These light sources include the sun, open flames, candles, torches, etc. But it was not until 1878 when the American Inventor, Thomas Alva Edison made the choice to start his experiment; we became familiar with what is termed, continuous sustainable light. This experiment made way to what we now called the light bulb.

Long before Edison perfected his invention, as you may imagine; he was faced with tremendous setbacks and experienced more than 1,000 failed attempts. Yes, you read it correctly, *One Thousand (1,000)* disappointments. In his own words, he said: "I didn't fail 1,000 times, I just figured out 1,000 ways how it could not work." No wonder he was able to invent the light bulb.

The **CHOICE** to not only possess a positive mindset like that but to maintain it speaks volumes about this man.

As you are reading these lines, what are the goals and dreams you have attempted, maybe once or twice and have given up on? Take the clues from Thomas Edison and get back to them. Maybe when you have tried a thousand times, you can cut yourself some slack. But before then be reminded that this is your goal, your dream and it is your responsibility to make it a reality; make the Choice to try again.

Use Your Frustrations To Motivate Your Choice

On my first trip to Florida, I got a chance to taste the well talked about espresso and muffin that is offered by Starbucks and experienced their ambiance. Before Starbucks became the place we go to have our business meetings and briefings, it was just a coffee - bean shop in Seattle. It was not until Howard Schultz intervened, that Starbucks became national and international recognized as it is today. Even though Schultz was not the one that started Starbucks, he is the person that is responsible for what it is today.
He was employed as a Marketing Director for the company and was sent on a trip to

Milan, Italy. While in Milan he became aware that, they were coffee bars on every street he visited. That awareness sparked something inside. Upon returning home, he went to his employers and told them of the idea he had to expand the company. Long and short of it, the owners refused and Schultz became frustrated. Unlike most people, his frustration did not just stay there. This frustration motivated him to make the choice to create his own business called Il Giornale. After operating a successful business for two years, he went back to his previous employers and acquired Starbucks for US$ 3.8 Million. He then renamed the Il Giornale to Starbucks and aggressively expanded the reach across the world.

So the next time frustrations carry dark clouds to engulf the sunshine that is in your dream, take clues from Howard Schultz and make the choice to do whatever it takes to make that seed grow to its full potential.

Thank you for making the CHOICE to reach out to me in this book. At this time, I am requesting of you to devote 20 years of your life in interviewing 500 people, all across the world. To conduct these interviews, you will need to provide your own income to cover your expenses for food and accommodation. Will You Accept?

If your answer was an instant YES, then congratulations; you possess the trait of the Rare Minority. (This will be discussed in the section **Identify Where You Are**.) In his bestselling book *Think And Grow Rich,* the American self-help author Oliver Napoleon Hill - stated that the above question was asked of him by the Steel magnate Andrew Carnegie in an interview. The answer to this question was what made way for the creation of countless successful individuals. Hill had the choice to say NO to interviewing more than 500 men for 20 years without pay or saying YES to devoting 20 years of his life to developing the philosophy of personal achievement. Even though the doubts and fear were present as Hill explained; he still made the correct choice, which undoubtedly changed the world in which we are now living. So the next time you are faced with a choice that seems daunting, take courage from Napoleon Hill to make the correct decisions and take actions for your Dreams and Goals.

3 IDENTIFY WHERE YOU ARE

It's a Friday evening. finally, the weekend is here. On an evening like this, if you are like most people, you could be on your phone rounding up the fellows and girls to meet up at your favorite chill spot or better yet, you could make the choice to catch up on some work you have been putting off. For me, I am making the choice to add at least a couple lines to complete this book; so it can inspire you to make the right choice for your dreams and goals.

I believe it is fair to say that all of us have dreams and goals, that is an absolute fact. So it is not only important, but it is also necessary to identify which of the group we belong to; whether the "**95 Percenters**" or the "**5 Percenters**".

If it is the first time you are hearing about this group, let me bring some clarity to it. The **95 Percenters** are those individuals, who are not living the life that they want; because of the poor choices that they have made and continue to make on a regular basis. They make up the majority of the population. On the other hand, the **5 Percenters** are those individuals who are living the life that they want, and are moving closer and closer each day to the attainment of their dreams and goals. They are the ones that are constantly making the correct choices, and they make up the minority.

Below you will find Traits of both the 95 Percenters as well as the 5 Percenters. I hope that you will look closely at these traits and make the choice to replace those that are found in the majority with those in the minority.

TRAITS OF THE MAJORITY - The 95 Percenters

1. **Procrastinate** - The habit of putting things off. Repeatedly making this choice will ultimately make your dreams and goals just wishful thinking. The next time you feel the urge to put off writing that book; getting enrolled in school; applying for that job; making that call, just remember that, **PROCRASTINATION IS THE ASSASSINATOR OF OPPORTUNITIES.**

2. **Doubt** - Having the feeling of uncertainty is quite natural. At some time or another, we all struggle with that feeling. However, giving power to your doubts - to make the choice of not doing what is necessary for the accomplishment of your dreams and goals is where the problem lies. Whenever this feeling comes over you, always remember that; you can either have your dreams and goals or you can have your doubts. You can never have both. So as usual, the choice is yours.

3. **Fear** - There are so many dimensions to this word, **FEAR**. Some say it is **False Evidence Appearing Real**, others say its **Forget Everything And Run**; both perspectives have their merits. But for me, Fear is nothing more than a state of mind. For example, if someone walks up behind you on a dark night, on a lonely street and poked something into your back and demand your cell phone. Your natural reaction would be fearful and corporate to the request because you **BELIEVE** that this

person is armed with a weapon and is going to hurt you.

But what if this was just a prank and the person only had a banana that he poked you with, and you were aware beforehand of this prank; then you would have had a totally opposite reaction. I emphasized the word **BELIEVE** because that is the **State of Mind** that you have chosen to be in.

Don't get me wrong here, the danger is **REAL**, but fear is just a state of mind. So whenever you are faced with a feeling of fear, that may be hindering you from taking actions for your dreams and goals; always remember that it is only a state of mind and with all state of mind you have the choice to choose.

4.   **Excuser** - At this very moment as I write about the Excuser Trait, I am currently at the laundromat waiting on my laundry. It takes about 45 minutes to get them all done. As I was leaving the house to go to the laundromat, I could have made the choice to leave behind my laptop; after all, I am just going to do laundry. However, I made the choice to not follow the excuser in me; but instead, I used the 45 minutes to add some meaningful information to carry this book closer to its completion.

They are so many people that will come up with so many reasons why they cannot achieve their goals and dreams. The more popular tracks on the excuser playlist are: I don't have money; I do not have the time; I don't have any support; I am not like this or that person and the list goes on and on and on.

Mark you, people can come with what I will call, *legitimate explanation* of why they can't make the decision for their dreams and goal. However always be reminded that the **best explanation is still an excuse**. Going back to the previous Trait of doubt; in life, you can either commit to your dreams and goals or you can commit to your excuses. Either way, it is a choice you must make.

5.   **Complainer** - This is a **HUGE** one, and if you are not careful this can be a part of your personality unbeknownst to you. I had a very close friend, she is ambitious; I mean she has big dreams and has great potential. Let us call her Sally. Sally would frequently message me and say, " Hey Omanzo I hope you are doing ok"; and I will respond and say, " I am doing GREAT." Then her immediate response would go something like "Lucky for you; I am here at work and I cannot stand the sight of these people." She would go on further to complain how unfair her boss was. Then after she will start complaining about her family, then she moves on to her boyfriend. She literally, when I say literally I mean LITERALLY- with a capital L, finds something to complain about in every aspect of her life. I hope that if you are like Sally, at this instant you make the choice to drop the habit of complaining.

6.   **Lack Of Confidence** - Lack of belief in oneself, is one of the major stumbling blocks that hinder one from achieving success in any calling. Often times this trait may have developed from way back when the individual was a mere child. As a child, it may have been challenging to make the conscious choice to have confidence. However, as we grow older and become aware of what we need to achieve; it is important that we make the choice to develop confidence in ourselves for the attainment of our dreams and goals.

7.   **Indecisive** - Today is February 27, 2018. Six (6) months prior to this date; I had made the choice that I would be submitting my resignation, to the company that I have been employed to for over 6 years. This resignation letter should have been submitted a month prior to this time. However, even though I knew what was to be done; this trait of indecisiveness had me a bit under wraps. To eradicate this trait, I asked myself the question; and you

can too whenever you are in a state of indecision. Are the decisions that I am going to make at this moment, carrying me to my dreams and goals? The answer for me was YES. Even though the trait of indecisiveness was present, I nonetheless made the choice that is in alignment with my dreams and goals. So I am letting you know that you too can also make that choice for your dreams and goals.

8.   **Lack Of Chief Aim Or Major Purpose** - I want you to pause for a moment and ask yourself this question. What is my CHIEF AIM in life? If you are like most people you probably cannot come up with a definite answer.

In one of the bestselling self-help books of all time - *Think and Grow Rich* by Napoleon Hill, which has sold well over a million copies since being published, Napoleon Hill states that in order to achieve anything worth achieving, you need to have DEFINITENESS OF PURPOSE. However, this is quite the opposite of the 95 Percenters lives. If you were to ask a 95 Percenter what is their CHIEF AIM or MAJOR PURPOSE in life, I give you my full 100 % guarantee they cannot tell you. My best bet is that they will ask why do you want to know.
I have asked that question more than a 1000 times and I have never gotten a definite answer. As a matter of fact, this is what I use most often to differentiate the 5 Percenters from the 95 Percenters.

If your answer was not definite as to what your chief aim in life is. Then you know which side of the curve you're on. However, I don't want you to stay on the 95% side and neither do you.
Identifying where you are is the first step.
The second step is to identify what is your major purpose in life and write it down.
And the third step is to simply make the choice each day

to take the actions necessary for the attainment of your purpose.

This is exactly what I am doing at this moment in writing these lines. I am taking action every day in writing this book. So as you read these lines, it will inspire you to take action needed to achieve your major purpose.

9.   **Negative Mental Attitude** - Only a few will admit to having this trait because it doesn't feel good to say that I have a **NEGATIVE MENTAL ATTITUDE**. If while reading this statement, you tried to convince yourself that you have neither a negative nor positive mental attitude. Then, my friend, I am so sorry to tell you that more than likely you possess the trait of a Negative Mental Attitude.

Let me reiterate. Identifying where you are on the curve is of paramount importance; so you can make the choice if needs be, to adjust your Mental Attitude.

Up to the present time of writing this book, I have only encountered one person that admits to actually possessing this trait.

I can remember inviting a young lady out to look at a business opportunity; and for weeks, for some reason or another she just could not follow up on her commitment to attend. Finally weeks later she told me that I should pick her up, so she could attend the business meeting. Before getting out of the car, she said I have something to tell you and I said go ahead.

She said, "I do not know if something is wrong with me, but I am a **Negative Person**. I always see the negatives in everything." This statement was shocking because it was the first time I have heard someone admitting to that trait, especially without being asked. I say that to say, that no one knows you more than you do, and to be fair to you; we all possess Negatives Mental Attitude at various times. Where the danger lies, is when it is the most dominant attitude and you are not being honest enough to realize that it is indeed present.

From time to time, I'll engage people in conversations to see how best I can inspire them to start making the choices that are necessary to accomplish their DREAMS and GOALS. Most times the conversations ultimately boil down to me saying, wherever you are at this moment are based on the choices you have made. Some will accept it and start making adjustments; yet others refuse to accept it, as you will see in the story that follows.

I once encountered a single parent mother with two kids. She told me that the kids' father decided he would not support her and the kids. So you can imagine when I told this lady that the situation she had found herself in was based on her choice. She got irate and said, "that's nonsense, that is ridiculous. You cannot tell me it was my choice to have my kids father leave me alone to support my kids." She went as far as to give me examples to support her point.

In case you are like this mother, let me do my very best to inspire you to see the truth in this statement. Because this is the only way you can start making the right choices for your dreams and goals.
I believe it is safe to say that all of us were basically born the same way; naked, scared and ignorant. Right? Let that statement soak in a bit. Some babies might be cuter than others, but the bottom line is that we all start out the same. From birth to wherever you are now, you can agree that you have made millions of choices whether consciously or unconsciously. Correct?
From the choice of your favorite attire to the choice of reading this book; was a choice right?
You absolutely didn't choose the infant school that you attended, that was most likely done by your caregivers. Before you say I am contradicting my statement, just

follow along for a while. The choice to attend that particular infant school was an unconscious choice made by you, that was forced on to you by your caregiver.

Following along these lines, let's go back to highlight the point that being a single mother was, in fact, a choice that was made. It was her choice to get into a relationship with the kids' father; it was her choice to get pregnant and have her children consciously or unconsciously. Everything that happened between the day she met her children's father up to the moment they separated was a series of choices.
Please note, that results come last. Your choices, however, those very small insignificant decisions come first. In the section on You Create Your Reality, I'll shed more light on this.

TRAITS OF THE MAJORITY - The 5 Percenters

1.   **Proactive** - " Even after thirty years of waiting, some will still be saying tomorrow. " These words from Sashin Govender really resonate with me. It stirred something within me to make the choice, to be proactive in doing my daily writing. Sashin is a very young, South African who is an international motivational speaker, trainer, and top income earner; who is all about teaching and bringing freedom to individuals all over the world.
He is someone that I will say is extremely proactive because he achieved all of the above accolades before reaching age 23. This is a huge accomplishment for anyone, no matter where in the world they reside. All of this was made possible, simply by choosing to be proactive. At the present time of writing this book, he has not even reached the age of 30; and yet he's already retired.

Making the choice to be proactive is a choice we all have to make in order to accomplish our dreams and goals; it is that simple. So I am imploring you to follow in Sashin's footsteps as well as the other 5% Percenters and make the choice to be proactive.

2.   **Confident** - Would you say that Sir Usain Saint Leo Bolt, Triple Olympic Gold Medalist, **World Records Holder** (Yes I said RECORDS Holder; because at the present writing of this book, he not only holds one or two but three World Records in the 100M Sprints, 200M and in the 4x100M), arguably a legend has confidence? Even if you are not a fan of athletics, you cannot dispute the fact that this legend indeed possesses the traits of the 5 Percenters, with the confidence he displays.

Before you say that Usain Bolt has everything to be confident about, perish that thought; and let us go way back before the world discovered him.

Usain was born and grew up in a rural community in the parish of Trelawny, Jamaica; nothing much to give him a confidence boost.

His confidence came long before any of us reading this book, saw him broke the world records. His confidence came first and his results followed after.

If you were to follow Usain's life, you will see that before every major championship there were always doubts, flying around the media and in individuals' minds. They did not believe he would be able to come out on top. However time after time from 2008 to 2017, Usain constantly made the choice to remain confident in his ability to make his dream of becoming a Legend a reality. His confidence always came through to prove the doubters and naysayers wrong.

What is that dream, that goal, that idea, that vision you

have inside you?

Is it starting a business? Is it writing a book? Is it getting in shape? Is it starting your foundation? Is it having a better relationship with your family? Is it Building your home? Whatever your dreams or goals are, I want you to stop right at this present moment and make the choice to be confident, and then take immediate actions to make them a reality.

3.   **Risk Takers** - Show me someone who is highly successful or a high achiever and I'll show you a **Risk Taker**. I strongly support risk-takers; because if there weren't any Risk Takers, the world as we know it today wouldn't be the same. As a matter of fact, you would not be reading this book at this moment if it was not for risk takers. If your parents refused to take the risk of having unprotected sex, then you would not be here. So the next time the thought of doing something for your better good, but it seems risky; remember that you are here right at this moment, because of the risk your parents chose to take.

Please do not misconstrue taking risks as gambling, because they have entirely different meaning. At this time, let me differentiate them both. Gambling is simple you investing your resources, most times money into something that you **cannot control the outcome**; For example, purchasing of a lottery ticket. You the buyer have no control over the numbers that will be drawn. On the other hand, a risk is the complete opposite of gambling. A risk is you investing your resources, where you **can control over the outcome**. For example, you pay for your college education; you have control of the outcome. Simply by ensuring that you attend the classes required plus doing what is required to pass the various courses. If all of the above has not inspired you to embrace the choice of being a risk taker, remember the following: having children is **risky**, getting married is **risky**, life is so **risky** that we are guaranteed, we are not going to make it out alive. So make the choice and take the risk to create the life you always wanted.

4. **Awareness of Their Chief Aim or Purpose** - Becoming aware of your chief aim in life or stated in another way; your purpose in life makes failure, not an option. Even though you may experience setbacks and temporary defeat; success is the only option, so long as you are aware of your purpose. Your purpose is what will get you out of bed every day. Your purpose is what will make you overcome whatever challenges that will come your way. Your purpose is ultimately the reason for existing.

Just in case you missed the story at the beginning of this book about the great inventor, Thomas Edison. He invented the incandescent lamp - what we all now know to be, the light bulb. These days many of us take this invention for granted because we are not aware of the story behind it.

Before accomplishing the invention of perfecting the light bulb, he tried **1,000** times. Yes, you read it correctly; he tried **1,000** times. How many of us would have stopped after the first try, or the tenth, much less to go a far as a **1,000**?

Thomas Edison had a purpose, and it was this purpose that drove him to make the conscious choice of surmounting setbacks after setbacks until his purpose was materialized.

As we identify our dreams and goals, it is not only necessary; but it is absolutely important that we choose to put back of it our purpose. Because it is with this purpose that our dreams will indeed become a reality. Make the choice and follow in the footsteps of Sir Thomas Edison to live by your purpose.

5.   **Positive Mental Attitude** - Most people will say that having a Positive Mental Attitude is easier said than done, and I am in total agreement. Most people are the same ones that possess the traits of the Majority - the 95 Percenters that was outlined earlier.
I believe you, on the other hand, are not most people, as a matter of fact. You are the rare Minority; the 5 percenter because you have made the choice to invest your time in reading this book. Please rest assured, that it can be developed - by making a deliberate choice to practice it.
Practice makes perfect, right? No that's not true, no one can never be perfect. **Practice makes Improvement.**

If you have lost a loved one, or specifically a mother you will understand the story that follows.

It was Thursday, December 14, 2017, at approximately 5 PM. A young man received a missed called from his sister. Upon returning the call, all he heard was crying and weeping on the other end of the call. At that time he thought the worst; because he had never heard his sister in that state before. Also, his mother was admitted to the hospital a day prior to receiving this call.
He braced for the news; that his mother, the woman that carried him into and through this world, the woman that made so many sacrifices to ensure her 9 children - in his mother's own words, "**PASSED THE WORST**", the woman that made it possible for you to be inspired after reading this book; had suddenly passed.
Even though as you can imagine, this very was devastating; he had made the choice to be strong and console not only his sister but the other family members and friends that were grieving. The following day was a work day, so he called and informed his supervisor of what had happened. His supervisor advised him, he should take the time off

and not report to work. However, he resisted the recommendation and showed up for work anyway.

At work that day he was still jovial and positive, even at his mother's funeral he still displayed that positive and jovial spirit. In case you haven't figured out who is this person - he is the author of this book.

What is startling, is at this very moment while I'm typing these words, I am sitting right at my son bedside in the hospital; cheering him up. I say all this to say; that if I could do it, then you can too. It all comes down to one thing – **THE CHOICE**.

Worrying or **stressing** about anything in life will not change the outcome; **they are just wasteful emotions**. Go back again and reread it. **Worry and Stress are just wasted emotions**. These emotions will never change anything. My best bet of what these wasted emotions will do - is to put you in a state of depression.

So make the choice to develop a **Positive Mental Attitude**; it is key to helping you to achieve your dreams.

6.   **Make Decisions Quickly** - It is said that, the speed at which you make a decision will determine your success. If you do not believe that statement, please read the story of the meeting between Napoleon Hill and Andrew Carnegie.

As a young man, Napoleon decided he wanted to get involved in law. However, the money to make his dream a reality was not forthcoming. So he devised a plan to start interviewing successful individuals, to have their stories published as a means of getting income needed to assist him with law school.

His first interview was with the Industrial Magnate Andrew Carnegie, one of the richest men in the world at the time. Andrew was so intrigued by young Napoleon that he told the young lad in his own words, "I want you to develop and take the **Philosophy of Personal Achievement** to the world; I need you to devote 20 years of your life to go and study over 500 individual successes and failures. You will do this with only letters of recommendation from me. Your daily expenses will be provided by yourself. Will you accept Mr. Hill?"

In less than 30 seconds the young lad accepted the challenge. It was that quickness of decision that created millions of successful individuals across the world directly and indirectly. As a matter of fact, if it was not for that decision you would not be able to be reading this book. Because it is through the reading of several books that Napoleon and many other authors have written that I found my purpose.

Making Decisions Quickly is just one part of the process in achieving success; making the choice to stick to that decision until success is attained is as equally important.

Henry Ford is the best person who I can use to illustrate the point of **stick-to-itiveness**. He became famous for developing the V8 engine. In case you have no idea what that is. Let me say, he was the first to cast 8 cylinders in a single engine block. If you're still confused, I am giving you the permission to stop reading and google what is a V8 engine. (Welcome Back !!) Before the V8 engine was created Ford went to his engineering staff and told them he needed to have 8 cylinders cast in a single engine block. The engineers said that it was impossible; then Ford replied I want it anyway. After a year of trying the engineering staff still report we have tried all we could, but this is impossible. Ford responded, "I don't care I need it done." After sticking to the task which seems so impossible, they finally made the impossible possible. This invention not only pushes Henry Ford way ahead of his time, it changed entirely how cars are manufactured to this day. So please be reminded of these two stories, the next time you are faced with making a decision for the betterment of your life. Make the Choice to make it quickly then stick to it until it is manifested.

7. **Choose the Right Association** - As I was pondering, what should I write about on the topic of choosing the right association; it came to me when I least expected it. I was in my office attending to a customer, then I overheard the statement, "don't be hanging with no jank-ass jokers that don't help you shine"; coming from the waiting area. That statement hit me like a bullet. As I listened keenly on the message, it became apparent that this was the voice of, "The Fresh Prince of Belair" - Will Smith. I immediately made a note of the statement, to retrieve it after I left the office.

Upon leaving work, that afternoon. I went online to locate the full message and it goes like this.
"I just saw this Rumi quote that I love – 'Set your life on fire. Seek those who fan your flames,'" Smith said. "The Philly translation of that is, **don't be hanging with no jank-ass jokers that don't help you shine**. The prerequisite for spending time with any person is that they nourish and inspire you. They feed your flame."

"Look at your last five text messages. Are those people feeding your flames, or dousing your fire? Put your phone down for just a second and look around. Look to the people around you. Are those people throwing logs on your fire -- or are they pissin' on it?

"The people that you spend time with are going to make or break your dreams. Everyone does not deserve to be around you. You've got to defend your light with your life. So who are the people in your life that are fanning your flames?

I don't believe I need to say anything else on this topic of choosing the right association. I could not have made it any clearer or concise or simpler than Will Smith. Many of us fall into the trap of only believing associations are only with people who are in our physical environs. However please be warned; we associate with others through books, audios, the radio, television, social media, etc. This is where yet another danger lies. Many of us are so caught up in the media with whose hot or whose not. Yet many more are unaware that the time they used for so-called CHILLING is in fact, a form of association.

If you are completely honest, you can agree most times this form of association is not inspiring at all. I can hear you saying, "all work and no play makes Jack and Jill a dull boy or girl;" and trust me I am in total agreement.

The fact though is if you neglect to associate with the right people; whatever dreams or goals that you desire will always elude you. So, as usual, the choice is yours. Make the choice to not only associate with the right people but also ensure you are associating with the right environment and anything that are pushing you towards your dreams.

4 YOU CREATE YOUR OWN REALITY

" You really mean to tell me, that I create my own reality?" Yes, without a shadow of a doubt I do mean it, that you create your own reality.

"That is crap, bull, nonsense, not true, stupid - You absolutely do not create your own reality; circumstances are what create your reality." This is the conversation that often takes place with the typical person.

If for some reason you are a 95 Percenter and aspire to become a 5 Percenter, you have the choice to make use of the advice that is outlined in this book. If not you are free to remain a 95 Percenter. After all, it is your life or in other words, it is your choice.

If you are still having a challenge in accepting the fact that you indeed create your own reality, please read this profound quotes by Mr. Earl Nightingale as slowly as possible and let it marinate for a while. **We are all self-made, but only the successful will admit it.** I need not write another word, because I believe Mr. Nightingale has driven the point home.

Before getting the inspiration to write this book, I can recall a conversation with a friend via WhatsApp messaging. It went something like this.

Friend: Well, some of us are richer than others lol
Me: Being rich is a Choice.

In the same way that being poor is a Choice

Friend: Really! If Rich is a Choice

Please tell me, how to get rich?
Me: Well, you can be rich by following the principles that lead to riches.

It is that simple.

Neglecting to follow those principles brings poverty.

Friend: What are those principles?
Me: You can start by reading this book, Think and Grow Rich by Napoleon Hill

Or for starters, start with this simple 30 minutes audio, The Strangest Secret In The World by Earl Nightingale

(A YouTube video of the audio by Earl Nightingale was sent.)

Friend: Ok
Me: However only 2 out of every 100 will listen.

The other 98 will find excuses.

For example, some will say I have no data service; I do not have the time; Not right now; Plus a whole sort of other excuses.

If any of those thoughts came to your mind, you will know which side of the scale you choose to be on.

Friend: True
Me: So it comes down to a choice

Prove to yourself that you want to be rich and stop whatever you are doing and listen to the YouTube video link above.

Friend: I am in a cab heading out of town.

So I will watch it when I get back home.
Me: Another excuse.
Do you have your headset/headphones?

Friend: It cannot be an excuse when you have bad eyes like mine.
I can't even text too long while I am driving.
My eyes hurt.

Me: Lol, It is an audio recording.
Your ears are what is needed, not your eyes
We can make the choice to commit to our results or make the choice to commit to our excuses.
Please remember the best explanation is still an excuse.

At the moment of writing this book, it has been over 2 months since we had the above conversation. I decided that I would follow up with her re the statement that she made above. She said that she would listen to the audio when she got home. As I said before - this has been over 2 months. So I thought, after all that time she must have gotten home at least once right?
See below, the follow-up conversation:

Me: Great Morning, I hope all is well on your end.
How was the audio?
Friend: Good Morning, I am ok. What audio?

Me: The audio I sent to you about 2 months ago, regarding the principles of getting rich.
Friend: Oh, I do not want to be rich. I just want to be content.
The audio was good.

Me: Ok great.
What did you get from listening to it?

Friend: Well, from listening to the audio. I now know that for me to be successful, I need to be focus, and take steps to achieve my goals. I have also started to listen to other motivational videos, and they are helping me a lot.

Me: That is great. Just keep on listening to these individuals and before you know it, you will be amazed. Just keep making positive choices.
Friend: Thank you will do.

I must say that I was shocked and quite rightly so because I did not expect her to respond the way she did. I am however happy that she shocked me. She not only listened to the audio that I sent to her. But she went further and made the choice to start feeding her mind with other positive information. As long as she keeps this habit up of making these positive choices, she will without a doubt create the reality that she desires.

If you truly desire to create the life you wanted. Please take a moment to answer the questions, not for me but for yourself.

Are you where you want to be, as it relates to your life?
Are you happy with your life?
Is your environment working for you?
Are you working on your dreams and goals?
Are circumstances working in your favor?

If the answer to any of the above question is no, then I am suggesting you pause and ask yourself; what is the cause of it. Stop!! Really stop and ask yourself what is the cause of it. If you are completely honest with yourself, you will discover that it all boils down to the choices that you have made, whether consciously or unconsciously. Your choices create your reality. Please note, it is a known fact that your results come last; it always comes last. If at this moment you are experiencing a negative reality, it is because of the negative choices that you have made. So it quite simple if you need to have a positive reality, result or outcome, just start making positive choices.

Take for example a man at 25 years old, he weighs over 300 pounds and all his family members are overweight.
Our first assumption will be. Oh, he is overweight because he hails from a big bone family, which is by the way nonsense.
If you were to look at the skeleton of that man as opposed to another 25 years old man who weighs 160 pounds. Their skeleton structure is almost the same; neither bones are bigger than the other.
The only difference is the choices for the food that they choose to partake as well as their health consciousness during the past 25 years of their lives.

In the original best seller, *As A Man Thinketh* by James Allen. James states that circumstance does not make the man, it reveals him to himself. He went on further to say that a man cannot directly choose his circumstances, but he can choose his thoughts, and so indirectly, yet surely, shapes his circumstances. Stated in another way, your choices are what creates your circumstances. " Wait, hold up and pause and answer me this; you are telling me that getting out of my bed at 4 am every morning, commuting for over 4 hours to a job I do not like, for the pay I do not want, standing the entire day, to only get 30 minutes break, if I am lucky - are the circumstances I created?" Yes, Yes, Yes, and Yes.
You created that circumstance. But the great news is that you can change that circumstance or any other circumstances whenever you are ready. By simply making the choices that will shape the circumstances you desire. Make the choice for your better future.

4 SUCCESS IS A CHOICE

Success means many positive things. Owning your home, having your own business, driving that fancy car, having a great marriage, having financial freedom; success is basically the goal of life for all those who have the courage to pursue it.

Before I go any further, let me just define what success means to me. Success for me can be defined in two ways:

1. Success for me is not how much money I can accumulate neither is it my bank balance. Success for me goes way deeper that. Success is how many lives I can touch to have them, in turn, achieve success. As a matter of fact, the purpose of writing this book is to inspire you to be successful in whatever area of life that you desire.

2. Success is the progressive realization of a worthy ideal. This statement came directly from, "The Strangest Secret by Earl Nightingale." That statement is so simple, yet so profound. In case you have missed its simplicity, it states that success is a process of accomplishing a goal and not necessarily the end result. For example, making the choice every day to read 10 pages of a book that will empower you to accomplish your goal, that is success. Making the choice to work out 30 minutes each day to keep fit is success.

Finding your Purpose

We can all agree that success is a choice. We can also agree that having a purpose will make it easier for us to make the necessary choices in fulfilling that purpose. So let us take the time now to identify your purpose.

All we need for this exercise is a piece of paper, a pen or pencil, and your mind. I hope your mind is already located, so stop and go locate a pen and paper.

My mentor Napoleon Hill through his book *Think and Grow Rich* told me to, write down the following and read it aloud before I go to sleep and when I arise. Now I am asking you to do the same. Write them down and read to yourself aloud each day as you arise and just before you go to rest. You can place it on your bathroom mirror, your refrigerator door, your bedside table, or wherever you will see it each day and just make the simple choice of reading it twice per day. Once you follow this instruction, you going to be surprised at how things begin to shift in your life.

A Quitter Never Wins and A Winner Never Quits.

Four Steps To The Habit Of Persistence

1. Definiteness of Purpose - Having a Burning Desire for Its Fulfilment.

2. A Definite Plan Express in Continuous Action.

3. A mind closed tightly against all negative thoughts and discouraging influences.

4. A friendly Alliance with one or more person that will encourage me to follow through with both my Plan and Purpose.

The first time getting these directives, I must say I was a bit skeptical. I asked myself how does writing down these lines and reading them aloud twice each day, will have any impact on me becoming successful. However, I did it nonetheless, and now I am happy I made the choice to do so.

At this moment I need you to do me a favor. Can you think of anyone you consider to be a high achiever? Do not be lazy now, stop for a moment and think. Now take a look at the list outlined. Does this individual that you have just thought about, followed all of the above steps outline? I am going to be bold and in your face and say, "Hell Yeah".
Any Individual that is considered to be a high achiever or making a huge impact on this world, from Jesus of Nazareth to Mahatma Gandhi has made the choice to follow these steps; whether they did it consciously or unconsciously.

If for some reason you still have a challenge in accepting the truth about those principles, let us test them against my favorite sprinter. You have guessed right - Usain Bolt. First though, let us really define these principles of success.

1. Definiteness Of Purpose - Having a Burning Desire for Its Fulfilment.

Defining your purpose is simple, but having a burning desire for its fulfillment is the challenging part. However, rest assured it can be developed.
To develop a burning desire, you have to know WHY you need to accomplish this purpose. What is your deep-seated WHY? It has to go further than, I just want to earn some money or drive a nice car or owning a home. Your WHY has to go way deeper.

It is said that, if your why doesn't make you cry, then your why isn't strong enough. Your why is what will cause you to go through failure after failure; it is the only reason why you place here on this earth.

2. A Definite Plan Express in continuous action.

Stop!!! Go back and please read over again? It did not say to just have a plan. It says create A Definite Plan, then goes on to further to say express that plan in **Continuous Action**. So the key in this statement is after we have identified our definite purpose, we then need to make the choice in creating a Definite Plan and continuously make the choice to take action on these plans.

3. A mind closed tightly against all negative thoughts and discouraging influences.

As we identify our dreams and our goals, often times our closest associates will bring the most resistance to what we are striving to achieve. Apart from our closest associates, we have a few silent enemies that are always lurking inside of us.
Those enemies are our doubts, our fears, and our excuses. What is important though is that as you are reading this statement, you are now aware of these enemies within.
So the choice is for you to close your mind tightly against all these negative thoughts and discouraging influences.

4. A Friendly Alliance with one or more person that will encourage me to follow through with both my Plan and Purpose.

No matter who you are; or how strong you believe you are. At times you will feel down as you pursue your dreams and goals. This feeling is quite natural and understandable. It is for this reason, that it is of paramount importance, that you align yourself with a friendly alliance - people cheering you on, people encouraging you when you feel like you cannot go any further. Making the choice to have these people in your life, will make your journey to the accomplishment of your dreams and goals, less stressful. Make the Choice.

As I have said before there is no one under the sun; who have achieved a high level of success. That has not consciously or unconsciously followed the principles outlined above. Now let us go back to my favorite sprinter Usain Bolt, to uncover if these principles hold true for him.

1. Definiteness Of Purpose - Having a Burning Desire for Its Fulfilment.

Usain Bolt's Definite purpose was to make a huge impact in the field of athletics. To achieve this, his purpose was to become a Legend.

2. A Definite Plan Express in continuous action.

His definite plan was to ensure that he wins all the major championship races. In order to win all his major championship races, he had to continuously keep his body in shape season after season, month after month, year after year. This means getting up early each morning for training, eating the right foods, saying no to immediate gratification, and the list goes on and on...

3. A mind closed tightly against all negative thoughts and discouraging influence.

If you have followed Usain's journey to becoming the legend that he is today. You would have seen that before every major championship competition, he was either plaque with injury or have some other competitor challenging his status.

These occurrences always spill over in media, casting doubt and having people wondering if he would be able to come out victorious. However, Bolt always had his mind so tightly closed against all negative thoughts and discouraging influences, with his mantra "**I Don't Think Limit.**" This propelled him to always do whatever that was necessary to be victorious at the end of each major championship.

4. A friendly Alliance with one or more person that will encourage me to follow through with both my Plan and Purpose.

Usain's friendly alliance came from many sources. However, two of those sources stand out the most. First his coach Glen Mills. Usain has said it many times that he was going to quit the sport, after not making the finals of his first Olympic Games. But through the encouragement of his coach and mentor Glen Mills, he remained in the sport despite his discouragements.

Another important person that encouraged Usain to follow through with his plan and purpose was, Nugent NJ Walker. NJ is Bolt's childhood friend and manager. No other person would have known Usain Bolt more than NJ, because of the many years they spent growing up in the hills and valleys of Sherwood Content, Trelawny, Jamaica. I can recall in March 2014 when I first met Usain, NJ was there at the airport in the background with him. I say this to say that NJ has been a major source of encouragement for Usain to become the Legend that he is today.

I could have used any great achiever to illustrate that their achievements are a result of the above principles outlined. But I do not think I have to, because I know you have grasped the point. So before you go, I want you to make the choice to follow the instructions that were outlined above, so one day you can walk up to me and say I have tried these principles and now I am living the life that I always dreamt of. As per usual the choice is yours.

5 FAILURE IS A CHOICE

Success leaves clues, and so does failure. At this exact moment, I am the 13th person - standing in the line of a well-known fast food restaurant. As I patiently wait in line to order a chicken sandwich, that my brother requested. I must say that the thought did come over me to order one for myself as well. This was however, the wrong choice - knowing that I chose to maintain a healthy lifestyle.

My mind went as far as to say "ok forget the chicken sandwich, but you can have some French fries and a soda - it's not like it's going to mess up your healthy lifestyle that much".

I wrote this to illustrate the point, that every second of our lives we are constantly being bombarded with choices to make. And if we neglect to make the correct choice, we indirectly make the choice of failure.

Today is Saturday, March 24, 2018, which marks the first day of leaving my day job; a job that I worked for over 6 years. Why did you do that, you may ask? Well, let me try my best to let you understand. Quitting a job that you are doing for 6 years I must say, isn't easy. A job which provides you with health insurance, pension, yearly bonus and the pay is great in comparison to other industries in the field.

You may be saying; you were brave, you had no responsibility, you were stupid, I cannot see myself doing that, it's just too scary.

But I will say, I made the choice to follow my passion; I made the choice to take the steps in the direction of fulfilling my purpose. If I had not made that choice. There would be no way you could be reading these lines - to inspire you to make the choices that are necessary to fulfill your dreams.

Continuing to answer the question of why I made the choice to quit my day job, can be found in this quote by a great philosopher. "**Insanity is doing the same thing repeatedly and expecting a different result**" put in my own dialect - The Jamaican translation "**Doing the same thing over and over and looking for a different results means you are a madman**".

Take for example, if your goal is to move from the state of Florida to Canada and each day with regularity, you make the choice to head south instead of north - you are indeed a madman.

Now let me put this all into perspective. For over 6 years I have been making the wrong choices, by going to a day job that is not in line in any way, shape or form to the fulfillment of my purpose. So I had no choice than to make the choice to correct my direction and set my sail to head north, in order to make my dreams a reality. If you are in a situation similar to where I was, where you are not heading in the direction of your dreams. I am saying to you right at this moment, please do yourself a huge favor - STOP! I repeat stop right now and then make the choice to change your direction to make your dreams a reality.

Thinking You Do Not Have a Choice is a Recipe For Failure.

Can you recall ever thinking or uttering the statement, "**I DO NOT HAVE A CHOICE OR I HAVE TO DO WHAT I HAVE TO DO?**" Well, if you are like most people I believe your answer is going to quite often. However, I'm going to be in your face and say, Yes!! you do have a choice. It doesn't matter where you are, or who you are; you always have the choice to change your circumstances.

Let me share a story with you that I hope will help you to start accepting the thought - that you do have a choice to change your circumstances.

I had a coworker, let us call her Joshy. Joshy was the one that gave me my first hands-on training in developing the skills as a Bank Teller. Prior to Joshy giving me those training, she had been at the institution for some 6 years as a Bank Teller. She didn't necessarily outright love her job; however, like most people, it was what paid her bills.

I can recall upon reading the book entitled, The Richest Man In Babylon - I suggest you make the choice and give it a read as well, it's a quick read and it will make a huge difference on your finances. After reading this book I was instructed that if I seek financial freedom, I should save at least 10% of my income. I immediately made the choice to follow the instructions to start saving 10% of every dollar that I earned. To not be selfish, I shared this idea with everyone I could, including Joshy. As you might have expected her response was that, she cannot save a dime from her income, because it just isn't enough. Being the person I am, I tried my very best to convince her that it can be done, so reluctantly she decided that she would commence saving 10% of her income starting January of the upcoming year.

At the present day of writing this book, it marks 2 years since Joshy and I had that conversation. However, she has still not made the choice to follow through on her commitment to setting aside 10% of her income. Even though in those 2 years; Joshy was the teller that received most of my bank transaction of the 10% of every dollar I earned, to place on my account. Each time as I make a deposit I encourage her and her responses is always more or less the same, "Omanzo I wish I was like you".

When I submitted my resignation, I informed her that I would be leaving in less than a month. Her response as usual was, "Omanzo I wish I was like you. I wish I was able to make the decision to resign as well - but I just can't." I told her that she does not need to be like me, but if she really wants to resign and go after her dreams the choice was hers to make. Deep down I could see that she understood that she indeed had a choice; however, she had neglected to make the right choice and now she's on the path of failure. I wish I could omit calling my dear friend a failure, but based on the definition of failure, her situation fits the bill.

Disclaimer: I am not telling you to just get up and leave your job, because I believe jobs are important. However, what I advocate is to create an exit strategy, if your job is not in line with your purpose.
If you are in a job that is not in line with your purpose, I suggest you specify a definite timeline when you plan to leave that job.
In my case, 8 months prior to resigning from my day job. I told myself that I will be leaving in 6 months time, which would have been January 31, 2018. However due to procrastination, a failure habit I must say; I went 2 months over the date I had specified.
What I did during those 8 months was to ensure, I made

the choices and take the necessary actions steps, of putting things in place to make my transition from leaving my day job to fulfilling my purpose, less stressful. I suggest you do the same, that is if you really which to make your life a fulfilling one.

Let me give you yet another story to ensure that you get the point, that **FAILURE is** indeed **A CHOICE.**

One Saturday morning at about 10 am I pulled up to a service station to get petrol for my car. I noticed that the pump attendant that was servicing, wasn't looking pleasant at all. She seemed pretty young, about 18 years old. In an attempt to see if I could remove the despair that was evident on her face. I engaged her in a conversation, which went something like this:

Me: Great Morning, what time did you start work today and when are you getting off?
Pump Attendant: I started at 6 this morning and I am getting off at 2:30 PM.

Me: Ok, cool. Let me have some gas.
 I am just curious. How long have you been working here?

Pump Attendant: Next week will make 3 weeks.

Me: That's Nice. Do you like your job?
Pump Attendant: No, I do not

Me: So why are you doing it?
Pump Attendant: I have to do it because I do not have any other choice.

At this point in the conversation, my brain went into overdrive and I started to explain to her that she indeed had a choice and she should refrain from believing that she doesn't have a choice.

This young girl like many other individuals is on the path of failure. If she does not wake up soon and come to the realization, that she has a choice in the job she is now doing. In a couple of years she will be in the same predicament as the Majority - The 95 Percenters, working at a job that they don't like, for the pay they do not want.

After driving off, I called my brother and told him about the conversation with the pump attendant. He told me that I should place this story in my book. I have made the choice to follow his advice and you are now reading the conversation.

I hope it will bring you to the realization that you have choices in every single aspect of your life; your job, your partner, your calling. There is no such thing as not having a choice. So now, choose to do what it takes to achieve success.

6 POVERTY IS A CHOICE

This topic is so challenging to write about and yet at the same time, it is so exciting. But before we go any further let us define **POVERTY**. Just by doing a simple google search on the meaning of poverty, you will see that it says, the state of being extremely poor. So let us go further and define poor. Again from a simple google search, it says that poor is lacking sufficient money to live at a standard considered comfortable or normal in a society. I apologize for going so basic in defining these keywords, but I do not want to run the risk of assuming that you indeed fully comprehend the meaning of the words poverty and poor.

Based on the definitions that you have just read above, it clearly defines my younger years. I was in poverty; I was in a state of being extremely poor.
In case you have missed reading the beginning of this book, let me share with you the level of poverty that I was in as a child.
Imagine if you may, waking up many mornings wanting to brush your teeth but having no toothpaste. Your only option was to run to the nearest corner shop to purchase not toothpaste as you might be thinking, but instead to

purchase table salt to brush your teeth. That was me. This happened so frequently because that was what my mother could afford. Sometimes she could not even afford the table salt. So the next option we had to take was to borrow table salt from our neighbor - under the pretense that it was for cooking. But deep down we know it was not for that reason. Talking about being in poverty, I was born in it.

I can go on and on with stories after stories about my struggles growing up, but I believe you get the overall picture, that I was indeed in poverty.

What change that state you may ask. Well, the answer is so simple you have read it so many time in this book. Yes, yes, yes, for the millionth time, it was just the choice I had to make to not be in that state.

In the opening of this chapter, I stated that this topic is really challenging to write about. This is due to the fact that I do not like the idea of calling anyone poor. However, the definition of poor, speaks for itself. If you are lacking sufficient money to live at a standard that is comfortable or normal in society, then you are POOR.

Why this topic excites me, is because I was in that state and I am aware of the choices that I had made from that young age, to "broke that grip" of poverty that was over my life.

If you are reading these lines right now and you believe that you are in a state of poverty, and you really wish to get out. Please stop at this instant, really stop and look back on all the choices you have made prior to this day. By doing so you will realize, where you had gone wrong. However do not stop there, instead I want you to start looking at the choices you can make from this day forward to "break that grip" of poverty over your life.

I can hear many of you saying, "Nice story, but you are not

in my situation, so you do not understand". I am going to pause and answer by saying; Yes, I do understand and I may not be in your exact situation but I do understand. As a matter of fact, if I were you I would have said the exact same thing. If I had your mindset; If I had experienced everything that you have experience; If I were YOU - then I would say the exact thing that you have said.

I hope you now understand that I do understand, so we can now move off that point and deal with what is most important. Which is, you taking the steps that are necessary to "break the grip" of being poor, so you can experience all the riches life has to offer you.

At this time let us take a look at a few of these individuals that were in poverty and decided that they were not going to accept that as their faith. They decided to make the choice to "break that grip". I deliberately use the phrase "break that grip", many times in this section for two reasons:

1. Repetitions yields results
2. I want it to become a part of your consciousness.

If the following persons could "Break The Grip", you can too.

Edwin C Barnes Rag to Riches

Edwin C Barnes was a master salesman, who became a millionaire at a very young age. This was made possible because of the choices he took to become the business partner of the one of the greatest inventor of his time, Thomas Edison. Before Barnes accomplished this feat, let us go back to see where he was and the choices that he had to make in making his dreams a reality.

In an article entitled " Bridge to Strength, Your Gateway to Success" by Robert Drucker, he wrote the following: "When he was a young man, Edwin C. Barnes yearned to become a partner of the greatest inventor on Earth, Thomas A. Edison. Even though Barnes was broke, had no special technical skills, and owned only meager clothes to wear, he pledged to himself that he would make his dream come true.

On a fateful day in 1905, Barnes rolled into West Orange, New Jersey on a freight train. Despite being poorly dressed and looking more like an outcast than a man of achievement, the Midwesterner walked into the famous Edison Laboratory full of confidence. There, he told the famed inventor that he had come to form a partnership with him. Nearby members of Edison's staff were amused by Barnes' declaration, and they laughed at him hysterically. But, Edison did not laugh. For, what he saw was a determined young man who was prepared to do whatever it would take to help bring new growth to his company."

It was that choice and confidence to take the first step in traveling to West Orange, to meet with Thomas Edison, that put everything in motion; even though he was not qualified at the time to be classified as a partner of Edison.

He did not accomplish his dream on his first meeting with Edison. He however, got something that many people would call failure. What he got was an opportunity to work as a floor sweeper in the Edison West Orange Complex. With this broom in his hand, he did the best work he could and make the choice to learn as much as he could about what made Thomas Edison tick.

Months and years had passed, without any sign of success in sight. In the mind of many, this would be a waste of time. But not in Barnes' eyes, he knew what his goal was and he was determined to be persistent until he accomplished it.

His time finally came when Thomas Edison invented the Ediphone (a device that captures the human voice with the capability to playback at a later time. This may not seem impressive to you at this time of reading, but be reminded this was the first time the human voice could be recorded and played back). Edison decided he wanted to carry this device commercial. However, his sales team at the time wasn't enthused about this device and didn't believe it could be sold commercially.

Barnes however, saw this as an opportunity and made the choice to not let this opportunity go to waste. He convinced Edison, that he will take up the offer to make this device commercial. Edison agreed and this decision made Barnes long-awaited dream a reality, to become the business partner of the great inventor Thomas Edison.

If at this time or any other time for any reason you find yourself in a challenging financial situation and you believe your dreams or goals are impossible, take courage in Barnes Rags to Riches story and make the choices that are necessary to make your dreams and goals a reality.

Timeline of A Poor Scottish Boy To The Richest Man In America

You would have seen me made mention of this name countless times in this book; Andrew Carnegie. Now let me shed some light on this Magnate. I have made the choice of using a timeline to illustrate the life of - **The Philanthropist, Industrialist, Entrepreneur, and Leader - Andrew Carnegie.**

Birth: On November 25, 1835, at Dunfermline, Fife, Scotland. Andrew made his arrival into this world. No one at the time could have imagined the impact that he would make on the world.

Migration to the United States: In Scotland, Andrew lived in a typical weaver's cottage with only one main room, consisting of half the ground floor which was shared with the neighboring weaver's family. His mother was forced to go to work to provide for the needs of the family because his father had fallen on hard times. To make matters worse the country was in a time of starvation. So in 1848, his parents were forced to make the choice to migrate with the family to the United States for a better way of life.

First Job: Andrew parents moving to the United State did not provide the promising results that were expected. Andrew had to make the choice to take up his first job as bobbin boy, changing spools of thread in a cotton mill 12 hours a day, 6 days a week in a Pittsburgh cotton factory.

Messenger Boy: In 1849, Andrew started to work as a messenger boy in a telegraph office and is later promoted to the position of telegraph operator.

Railroad: In 1853, he took a new job as the personal telegrapher and assistant to Thomas A. Scott, the superintendent of the Pennsylvania Railroad's western division.

Investment: Andrews's first investment was made in 1856 on the sleeping railroad cars. Two years later he began to receive about $5,000 annually. This was three times more than his salary from the railroad; not a bad choice after all right?
Side note - for those who do not make the choice to take time to understand investment; and in return do not make the choice of taking the risk to invest, take this as a lesson.

Wealth Accumulation: Unlike the majority, Andrew in the year 1861, made the choice to use money from his previous investment in the sleeping car business to invest in an oil company. This choice was what started his accumulation of true wealth.

Write Yourself a Letter: In 1868, Andrew wrote himself a letter which outlines all his plans for the future. This includes to resign from his business at age 35 and live on an income of $50,000 per year; devoting the remainder of his money to philanthropic causes and to devote most of his time to education.

First Steel Plant: Andrew continued to make the choice to accumulate more wealth so he could help those that were in challenging financial situations. This choice led him to open his First Steel Plant in 1875.

Rival Steel Company Purchase: As you can imagine with all business, you will have competitions. To remove that competition Andrew brought his competition, the Homestead Steel Works.

Carnegie Steel Company: In 1892, Andrew Carnegie made the choice to incorporate many technological innovations into the production of steel, under the name Carnegie Steel Company.

Carnegie Sells To Morgan: In 1901, Carnegie sold his steel company to J.P. Morgan for $480 million, this choice not only allowed Morgan to form U.S. Steel. This Choice made Andrew Carnegie at the time, the richest man in the world.

Believe it or not, you will have to agree to the fact, that whether these choices were made consciously or unconsciously, they were indeed the choices that move the poor Scottish boy Andrew, to become the Richest man and most ardent philanthropist of his time. I hope that you were inspired by the story of Andrew Carnegie and in return, you will make the choice to step into the light.

The Journey of A Strong Woman

Let us embark on a journey to learn who else triumphed over poverty by answering these questions:

Who do you know that has the birthday January 29, 1954?

Who do you know that wore potato-sack overalls as a child?

Who do you know that was born into poverty in rural Mississippi?

Who do you know that was molested at the age of 14 and became pregnant, and lost her in infancy?

Who is the strongest woman you know? (Please exclude your mom and yourself if you are a female)

Who do you know that is an American media proprietor, talk show host, actress, and philanthropist?

Who is the most powerful black woman you know?

Who is the richest African American according to the Forbes list?

Who do you know, to be the first Multi-billionaire black person?

I believe by this time, you have discovered who this woman is. But just in case you missed it. She is no other than the "Queen of All Media" Orpah Gail Winfrey, but we all call her big sister Oprah.

By popular belief, Oprah should not be the success she is today. This strong black woman has made the choice over and over again, to lift herself from poverty to becoming one of the most influential people of our time. I don't believe I need to go any further in this discussion, because I know we all know who is Oprah and I know you have fully grasped the point, that no matter you are or whatever poverty situation you have experienced or experiencing. You indeed have the choice just like Big sister Oprah to lift yourself from Poverty to Riches.

How To Overcome The Lazy Feeling.

To be fair with you, sometimes that feeling of laziness will most definitely come over you as you pursue your dreams and goals. I can promise you that. It may be getting out of bed to go to work,
It may be taking up the phone to make that prospect call, It may be getting up to study, It may be reading 10 pages daily of this book, It may be writing your own book. It may be… whatever you need to get done.

I believe you get the picture. As long as we are on this earth plane, we will have to deal with this feeling. However, If we are not careful, this feeling has the potential to lead us into a state of poverty. And I do not believe you or anyone for that matter deliberately wants to be in that state.

There is this condition, primarily associated with writing, in which an author loses the ability to write; termed writer's block. As I ponder on what to write this morning, that feeling of laziness came over me.

Ahead of me laid two choices. One (1), I could choose to not write today, which will go against my daily habit of writing and in turn delay the completion of this book - that you reading to be inspired to make the choice to step into the light. Or two (2), I could muster up the courage to write. Thankfully I made the choice to persevere.

How I mustered the courage is quite simple, and I suggest you make the choice to use it as well - whenever the feeling of laziness or any other negative feelings comes over you.

"**Motions are the precursors of emotions**". That is it, that phrase is what I used to overcome the feeling: very simple right?

But in case you might have missed it, let me make it clear. Before I go any further though, let me state for the record that this phrase was not developed by me. I actually heard of it while listening to an audio recording in the book, The Magic of Thinking Big by David Schwartz. It stated that you cannot control your emotions directly. They are controlled only through your choice of **Motions** and **Actions**. So the secret is not to focus on getting rid of negative emotions, but rather to make the choice of going through the desired "**motions or actions**".

Making that choice and taking actions will soon have you feeling the more desirable "**emotions.**"

Before wrapping up this section let me give two examples to illustrate the point that **Motions** are indeed the precursor of **Emotions**.

At the present day writing of this book, my fiancé's job is at a well-known hotel, in Manhattan, New York City. For her to get to work, she is required to travel by train and bus/cab for almost two hours.

She loves her job, but for the love of Christ, she hates the night shift.

She dreads the night shift so much, that literally every night when she leaves out to go to work on the night shift, she not only harbors thoughts of quitting but on numerous occasions, she's like "babe I cannot take this no more - I am quitting tonight". However as she completes her shift, she is then like "babe I change my mind, I am not quitting".

She went as far one night has to write her resignation letter, handed it in and then requested for the letter to be withdrawn. This goes to show you, how much she hated the night shift.

I can recall one night, she called and said "husband, I'm feeling so lazy and need to get up so I can go to work, please help me." The phrase "Motions are the precursors of emotions" flashed in my mind, so I repeated it to her.

Saying that phrase to her had no impact whatsoever because she was not in that receptive state. I did the next best thing by putting this phrase into action. Our conversation went something like this.

Me: Babe, I want you to put your feet on the carpet and tell me how it feels
Wife: It feels old.

Me: Ok, kool
Can you turn on the light, pull your door and please go into the kitchen for me.

Wife: I am in the kitchen

Me: Open the refrigerator to get some water to drink.
Wife: I do not need any water; I just need the energy to get up to get ready for work.

By this time the trick had already worked, because even though she did not need any water to drink. She was already on her feet in the kitchen and was already in motion, so all she needed was to do the obvious and get ready.

The second example that I am about to share, is about me. The night before I wrote these very words, I was out working all night and I didn't get home until some minutes after 7 am in the morning. Needless to say, I went straight to sleep. To say I was totally beat is an understatement.

Each time I tried to get up, that feeling of laziness kept on overpowering me, even though I had a lot of things to get done.

A phrase that I grew up hearing my father frequently used, flashed in my mind, "**Batty never say get up**" translate to "Your buttocks will never encourage you to get up when you have something you need to get done." It was that phrase that gave me the courage to write these lines that you are now reading.

After writing that phrase "Batty never say get up", I became aware that it was not only saying the same thing as the phrase, "Motions are the Precursors of Emotions" but it has the same power to drive anyone into action to make the choice, that is necessary to complete any task.

It is so simple, yet many people will not make use of it. If you are reading this at this moment make the choice to not be most people; instead, make the choice to get into motion to create your best life ever.

7 RICH I$ A CHOICE

If after reading the previous section that Poverty is a Choice. I would now want to believe, that you will accept or at least be receptive that being Rich is also a Choice. I wish I could bestow all the riches that you desire with the wave of a wand. But the reality is, I am not Harry Potter or any wizard for that matter. What I can do however is through this book and in these lines, do my utmost best to inspire you to make the choice to create a life of abundance - that you so rightly deserve.

Do You Want To Be Rich?

Before we go any further, may I ask you this question? Do you want to be rich? Stop!! I really want you to answer the question. Do you want to be rich?
I have asked this question so many times, and below are a few of the responses I have received. Please check if any of these hold true for you as well.

"I do not want to be Rich, I want to be comfortable"
"No I don't need riches; I just want to be content."
Oh, the Famous response "Rich People are not happy"

Yet a few will say "Yes! Of course, I want to be rich.

Now let us discuss a few of these responses.

I Do Not Want To Be Rich, I Want To Be Comfortable

I must admit that for many years, this was also my choice of response to the question of being rich. This response was adopted from my mother. For as long as I could remember, I kept hearing my mother repeating this statement, whenever the topic of wealth was brought up; "I don't want to be rich, I only need to be comfortable." The sad thing about this is that I too made the choice to subscribe to her belief, without even being aware.
However, as I got older I came to the realization that in order to be comfortable, then I had to make the choice to be rich.

Rich People Are Not Happy

I hate - yes I know that hate is a strong word, but I am letting you how disgust I feel about this response. I absolutely hate when people use the statement that you cannot be rich and happy. Accepting this statement as truth in your life, removes any possibility of prosperity that you so rightly deserve. If you are one of those people who is reading right now, please make the choice to pay close attention so I can help you step into the light - to become your best self.

To be Rich, Poor, Happy or Sad is a choice. A poor man can be happy right? Also, a poor man can be sad. A rich man can be also happy as well as a rich man can also be sad. So where does this fallacy comes from? I do not know and quite frankly, I do not care. What is important at this point in time, is that you understand that there is no correlation that riches removes happiness. Also at this moment, I want you to make a conscious choice to remove this fallacy from your brain and start taking action to achieve all that lives has to offer you.

Of course I Want To Be Rich

Base on the many persons, who I have had the courtesy of asking the above question of wanting to be rich. A few of them answered and said: "Yes Of course." However, the important question to be answered is not if you want to be rich. But instead, what are you doing to be rich? Whenever this question arises, I can never receive a definite answer. The answer I received most of the time is always more or less, that they are working on it. But as I push for more details, they can never say exactly what they are working on. At other times they may respond by saying I will start soon.

Please note that the **word soon is not a definite time**, let me repeat, the word soon is not a definite time. So if you are ever tempted to use the word soon as it relates to a time you need to get something done. Please make the choice to resist the urge and provide a definite time. By following this simple instruction, it will hold you accountable to get that task done in the definite time you have set.

In the following section, I will outline the principles for getting rich adopted from the book, " The Richest Man In Babylon" by George Clason. If you haven't read it before go give it a read, and if you have read it before go give it another read.

The following are the 7 lessons that any individual may use to achieve financial freedom. Let me emphasize it; the principles you are about to read below will bring you Financial Freedom, whether you are black or white, slim or fat, young or old or whatever state you might find yourself in - so long as you make the choice to put these principles into action immediately.

1. Pay Yourself First

The first lesson is for you to pay yourself, at least 10% of whatever you earn. Out of every dollar you earn, take out at least 10% and pay yourself first. It is that simple. I can hear many of you saying, I don't earn enough, so there's no way I can do that.

My question to you is how bad do you need financial freedom? If you really inspire to be financially free, I implore you to make the choice to put this principle into practice. A part of all you earn is yours to keep. It should be not less than a tenth, no matter how little you believe you earn. It can be much more as you can afford, but not less than 10%.

By making this choice consistently, it will develop a habit and you will be shocked as to why you haven't started this habit before.

2. Control Thy Expenditures

After you have paid yourself at least 10% of your earnings, you are then left with at least 90% for your earnings to cover your expenses. This is where the majority of us fall down, we focus solely on paying all our expenses and then attempt to pay ourselves after. But what you will find out to be true for most people, is that there is nothing left to save after they pay all their earnings on their expenses. Please don't get me wrong, by thinking I am advocating that you should not pay your bills. As a honest person, you should ensure that all your bills are paid.

However what I am advocating is that you make the choice to budget your expenses, so that you will be in a position to pay yourself first.

3.   Make Your Money Work For You.

From the money, you have saved by paying yourself first. This money should be used in smart and well-researched investments. Please be warned as it relates to investment or any subject for that matter "**ONLY TAKE ADVICE FROM PEOPLE** Who Are **QUALIFIED** to **GIVE y**ou **ADVICE**." To get advice ON investments, there are many self-help books that you can make the choice to get a hold of, to educate yourself on how to have your money work for you.

4.   Guard Thy Treasures Against Loss

If you have ever owned a motor car, you would have been made aware that insurance is necessary for safeguarding your treasure. In this case, safeguarding your motor car. So it is the same with the investment, you need to have insurance in place to protect your investment; to minimize the lost if needs be.

5.   Make Of Thy Dwelling A Profitable Investment

We all need shelter; we all need to live somewhere right? But the accurate question should be is your currently dwelling in a profitable investment? You might say, yes of course it is; after all, my home is an asset. But let me touch this highly debated subject at this time. Before that though let me differentiate between assets and liabilities in the simplest terms possible. Coming from the entrepreneur, investor and author Robert Kiyosaki in his book, Rich Dad Poor Dad. He defines an asset to be anything that puts money into your pocket and a liability as anything that takes money out of your pocket.

Based on that definition, the statement that our homes are our biggest assets does not hold true; if every month we are paying a mortgage to our banker, then it is indeed a liability instead of an asset.

To turn your home into an asset can be a bit challenging. But rest assured, it can be done by simply making the choice to do whatever it takes to lessen the expenses as much as possible for your home. You may also if you are not a homeowner as yet, make the choice to create an income stream that will cover the future payment for your home.

6.   Ensure A Future Income.

In ensuring a future income, this can be done by making the choice to follow the quote from Benjamin Franklin, "Remember that money is of a prolific generating nature. Money can beget money, and its offspring can beget more." I believe I need not say more.

7.   Increase Thy Ability To Earn.

If this is the only statement you understand from this entire book, and then make the choice to take immediate and continuous action to invest in yourself. I would be so grateful and happy to call this book a success.

The most important investment that anyone can make is not in oil, nor in real estates, nor in business but in themselves. I am imploring you right at this time to please make the choice, to make it a habit of continuously investing in yourselves, because it's the only way to experience the life you desire.

Make the choice to put the above principles into action, so your next 5 years will not be like the last 5 years. Make the choice now.

Is Financial Freedom Possible For An Employee?

Let me be really blunt as this time, even though you might not like my answer. However, this book is not about you liking what I am writing; its quite the opposite. It is about inspiring you to become your best self. So if that means I will have to step on some toes, then so be it. It is a choice I am quite happy to make.

It is a well-known fact, that Financial Freedom is not possible for an employee, if you doubt me on this then answer this simple question. Who do you know, that is an employee and is financially free? If by any chance you are able to provide me with a person who fits this description, could you please do me the honors of introducing me to them, so I may retract my statement or better yet find out how they achieved the impossible.

In order for us to be on the same page, let me define what I meant by Financial Freedom. Financial Freedom means you having enough wealth to live on without working.
I have made the choice to write about this topic because majority of individuals are being delusional, believing that someday they will attain financial freedom. Yet they have no plans in moving from being an employee to an employer.
Please note this section is not for the majority, if you wish to be an employee all your life and not experience financial freedom then you are free to stay there. However, do not expect one day that miraculously financial freedom will drop in your lap; to think so is to be insane.

To cut you some slack; an employee may experience financial freedom, if that employee were to make the choice to develop assets that will generate income (cash flow) that is greater than their expenses. So to make the heading of this sections foolproof; let me say, that financial freedom is impossible for a person who is solely an employee. If you are an employee reading these lines at this moment and you seek financial freedom, **make the choice** to not only accept what was said but make the choice to find means and ways to increase your assets (things that put money in your pocket) column. You can start that process today by reading or listening to the book, Rich Dad Poor Dad by Robert Kiyosaki.

Is Money The Root Of All Evil?

As I am writing these words, it is currently 8 PM. I am at the Norman Manley International Airport waiting to board a 1 AM flight to New York City, to surprise my fiancé and attend her Aunt's 60th birthday celebration (Side note best Aunt ever, she is the main reason why our relationship is where it is. She is also in on the surprise).

Unlike most people who would just sit and wait; and do nothing constructive for the next 5 hrs. I have made the choice to use some of that time to add at least a couple more lines to this book, so you are able to be reading it at this moment.

Getting back to the question at hand: Is money is the root of all evil? What is your take on this question? Is it really the root of all evil? Just before I wrote this line I asked the question to someone who was waiting in the airport as well and her response was, "No! That's ridiculous, money is not the root of evil. I believe the evil has to do with the person who possesses the money." I am also of this same view. How can money by itself be evil? Money is nothing more than a mere piece of paper or coin that has a value, so there is no way that money by itself can be evil. I believe it has to do with what it is used for, which can either for good or for bad.

Some time ago, I was at a seminar and I heard the speaker said the following and it stayed with me to this day. "The true definition of the word perversion is using what was meant for good for bad." This warrants a repetition, "The true definition of the **PERVERSION is USING what was meant for GOOD for BAD.**" He went on to cite a few examples. Take for example, fire can be used to save lives as well as take lives. Water can be used to save lives as well as to take lives. If these examples hold true then the converse holds true as well, that Money can be used to take lives as well as save lives.

So where did we get our teaching or knowledge that money is Evil? Many will argue and say that the Bible says, money is the root of all evil. However, let us take a closer look at the scriptures. In 1st Timothy 6:10, it states that for the LOVE of Money is the root of all evil. The keyword here LOVE, not just money itself.

Before I wrap up this section, if we are all honest with ourselves we will all agree that money is important in the economy we live. As a matter of fact, we were sent to school and trained to work for money and likewise, we do the same thing to our offspring. However, there is little or no education about money that is taught in schools. No wonder why the majority of people believe that money is evil, because of the lack of knowledge on the subject. In closing let me share my opinion on this topic, I do not believe that the love of money is the root of all evil. I believe it is the lack of thereof.

So at this point as you are reading, I want you to make the choice to start the process of educating yourself about money, so you will be able to make use all the things that money can buy.

Best Definition of Rich

You may be asking yourself, why did I wait all the way to the end of this section to define Rich and why should you accept this definition? Fair questions both. I waited until this moment to define what it means to be rich for 2 reasons. 1. I really have no idea why I waited to the end to define Rich and 2. again I have no idea why I waited until the end to define what it means to be rich. Hope you get the humor. Why should you accept this definition you ask? Well, please bear with me for a moment and continue reading and it will become clear to you, why you don't have any choice than to accept this definition as true.

Let me ask you a question that I have asked countless of other individuals. Do you want to be Rich? If your answer is yes, then great. I want you to be rich.
If you answered no or anything along that line, like many other individuals, then please answer the following 12 questions Yes or No. These 12 questions were inspired by my Mentor Napoleon Hill on what he termed, the 12 Riches of Life

1. Do you want a **Positive Mental Attitude?**
2. Do you want to possess **Sound Physical Health?**
3. Do you want to have **Harmony in Human Relationships?**
4. Do you want to have **Freedom From Fear?**
5. Do you want to have **Hope For Achievement?**
6. Do you want to have **Capacity for Faith?**
7. Do you want to possess **The Willingness to Share Your Blessings?**
8. Do you want the ability to **Labour for Love?**
9. Do you want to have an **Open Mind on All Subjects?**
10. Do you want to have **Self Discipline?**

11. Do you want to have the **Ability To Understand People?**
12. Do you need **Economic Security?**

Was the answer to any of those questions Yes? I believe so. Hence you indeed want to be rich. This is what I use to measure what it means to be rich on this Earth. If you were to take a close look at the list of questions, you will see that economic security comes last on the list of questions.

Economic Security is placed last on the list of questions intentionally. Unfortunately, most believe riches only refer to material possessions or money. This way of thinking is most detrimental. But if you really want to be great I am suggesting you make the choice to include at least a couple, if not all of the above list as well in your definition.

As this chapter comes to a close I want you to make it a mandatory choice, to use every second of every minute of every day to be rich.

8 MAKING THE CHOICE FOR EDUCATION

"I do not have the time", "I am not smart enough", "I have a family to care for"," I just can't afford it." Those are just a few of the reasons people believe are preventing them from having the education they need. So at this time let us look at these reasons individually. If by any chance any of these applies to you, I hope after you have gone through this section you will be inspired to make the choice to overcome whatever reasons that are standing between you and your educational goals.

1. I Do Not Have The Time To Pursue My Education

This is not rocket science, it is simply common sense. We all know that there are 24 hours in every day. From the Janitor to the President of a major cooperation, we all have the same 24 hours. So where does this come from to say that we don't have enough Time? This is nothing more than just an excuse.

I believe if you absolutely need to gain knowledge in any

subject area, you will make the choice to prioritize your time to pursue your education. So the next time you feel like taking refuge in the alibi, of not having the time to pursue your education or to pursue anything for that matter. Catch yourself and remember that it is not true, you have all the time you need like everyone else. You just need to make the choice, to use your time wisely to make your dream a reality.

2. I Am Not Smart Enough

Saying to yourself, that you are not smart enough is counterproductive to you attaining your educational dreams and goals. Isn't that the reason you decided to pursue your education, so you may become smart? Of course, it will make you smarter. Maybe not the smartest in the world, but definitely you will acquire some amount of knowledge that will make you more educated than before. Read the following section below and then, make use of the lessons that it has to offer you in shifting your mindset from believing you are not smart enough.

You Become A Pro In Anything You Put 10000 Hours In

Those were the words I received from my brother, some 3 years prior to me writing this book and I am now passing them on to you.

You can make the choice to reject it, or you can make the choice to accept it.

For me, I have made the choice to accept and apply it to learning photography.

I can recall the first time holding a DSLR camera to take a photograph. I was not able to locate the button that I should press to capture the photograph. You might be saying that is silly, everyone must know which button to use. If that was your thought, you obviously have never been exposed to a DSLR camera.

In the beginning of learning photography, I made it my choice to watch a chapter every day on the Foundation of Photography. At that time, I did not own a DSLR camera. But I did not allow the lack of a DSLR camera to hinder me from making the choice to put in the hours necessary in becoming a pro. For the record, up to this present day of writing, I am nowhere close to 5,000 hours, much less 10,000 hours. However, I have come a very far way in photography, where I can say I was able to capture a wedding all by myself. So if for some reason you believe you are not smart enough in an area you want to pursue, just make the choice to start putting in the time necessary - whether you have all the resources are not. By making this choice, you will be surprised at how smart you will become. Make the choice to put in the time that is needed to becoming a pro.

3. I Have A Family To Care For

Whether you have a family to care for or not. Do you believe if you are successful in attaining the education you choose to pursue, it will help you to take better care of your family? Without a doubt, of course, it will.
Far too often you will observe individuals that start a family, make the choice to procrastinate on their goals, especially their educational goals. This type of procrastination is quite understandable. However, I am suggesting that if you really want to accomplish your dreams and goals in creating a better life, for not only you but for your family as well. You need to make the choice to not allow yourself to put off things today because of family reasons. Making this choice will bring you further away from providing for your family than you think it will. So if you are the person, who believes in putting off your educational dreams or any dreams you have for that

matter. I want you to take the lessons from what you have just read, then make the choice to drop this alibi and take the necessary actions in the attainment of your goals.

4.   I Can't Find The Money For My Education

That was exactly what my thoughts were, as I pondered over the thought of going to college. I hope by the end of my story, you will be inspired to make the choice to pursue your educational goals.

In 2005 after completing my high school diploma, I knew exactly what I wanted to pursue. I knew that I wanted to study at the University of Technology to obtain my Bachelor's Degree in Computing and Information Technology. I had all that was needed to make this dream a reality, expect one. You guessed it, I couldn't find the money. If you've been following from the beginning of this book you would have been aware that my father had retired from the year 1998. And as for his pension, it could not even cover food for the family. You would have been also made aware that my mother was also not in any possession to come up with the money, that was needed for me to pursue my educational dream.

People Are Placed In Your Life for A Reason

While in my 4th year of high school my twin brother applied for a few summer jobs. He was successful with two of the jobs he applied for. I, on the other hand, was not so successful. However, being a twin has its benefits. Seeing that my twin brother could not work the two jobs at the same time, I made the choice to work under his name in one of the jobs. Because we are identical twins, the employment agency did not have any clue of what took place. I was placed to work with a lady by the name of,

Mrs. Minette Anderson-Myers, I really love and appreciate this lady so much. As you read, you will see why. We worked together for three weeks where we got to know each other a bit, except that she called me by my twin brother's name, Olando.

I met up with her a year after; at this moment, I had already completed high school and was working at a supermarket, packing bags. She came up to the counter and greeted me and invited me to attend church with her. I accepted the invitation and attended church the following Sunday. I even came clean and explain to her that I am a twin and my name is actually Omanzo and not Olando, as well as the whole summer job shenanigans. I guess maybe the Lord spoke to me that day in church.

After church she invited me to her home for dinner; this marked the inception of my Sunday routine. Every Sunday, I would attend church and then go to her home for dinner. This created a huge bond between us, to the point where many people thought she was my mother.

One specific Sunday evening after church, she enquired what were my plans as it relates to furthering my education. I told her I did not know; which was a lie. Because I knew that I wanted to attend the University of Technology. I was just too shy, so saying that I did not know seems like the easiest response to avoid having a conversation. She then asked about my qualifications; upon informing her she said exactly these words. I will never forget, "Omanzo, I need you to apply for college and I will be your guarantor for your student loan." I was so humbled because, at that moment, I saw the possibility of making my dream of attending the University of Technology; and attaining a Bachelor's Degree in Computing and Information Technology, a reality.

I followed suit, applied for the programme of my choice as

well as for student loan. When the time arrived for her to sign the student loan document, she had the choice to sign for one (1) year at a time or for the entire four (4) years. She did the latter. I do not know if she knows how much I appreciate her doing that for me. That choice that she made, removed the pressure from me trying to seek a guarantor every year, so I could focus all my energy on completing my college degree.

The Choice To Swallow Your Ego

The University of Technology approved my application and so did the Student Loans Bureau. I was all set and ready for college in less than a week. Until I received a mail stating that students who are using student loans to cover their college fees needed to pay an auxiliary fee amounting to about $23,000 JMD, equivalent to 200 USD before they can commence registration. You may be thinking, that is not a lot of money. However, this was in the year 2006, where no one in my family was employed. So this was a hefty sum to come up with on such short notice, of one week.

I was frustrated and I could not see any way of coming up with that money; I made the choice to defer my application to the following year. By doing this, I could get a job, worked and save so I would have more than enough to cover the auxiliary fees the following year. I actually wrote the letter and went to my friend house to get it printed. At my friend's house, I was talking to his mom about deferring my application to the next year, because of the lack of money to cover the fees in such a short time. She listened and made a few suggestions, which I didn't like because of my **ego**.

Side note: What do you want more, your **Ego** or your **Dreams**? The choice is yours.

Even though I had that ego, I made the choice nonetheless. I made the choice to follow through on my friend mother's advice to go to the members of parliament office to seek assistance. As I said before this was not something I wanted to do. However, I am telling you at this moment that I am so happy that I made that choice. This choice did not only allow me to get the money for the auxiliary fees, but it provided me with so many opportunities for jobs and connections throughout my entire time at college and after.

Never Give Up (Who Have Raw Meat Seek Fire)

On your journey in accomplishing anything worthwhile achieving, you will undoubtedly meet oppositions and rejections. To not think so is just naive. Even though the challenges will come, you have the choice to not be subdued by them.

In my second (2nd) year of college, I applied for a scholarship and was rejected. I received a well-written email. Stating that, "it is with much grief that after reviewing your application we regrettably at this time informing you that your application was not shortlisted to be approved for the named scholarship." Reading that email did not sit well with me. There I was thinking, someone who is trying is best to get his college degree so he could better himself; has just gotten rejected. At that moment, I could've made the choice to accept rejection and feel sorry for myself, like countless of the other individuals who were turned down for the scholarship or I could make the choice to at least attempt to do something about it.

I can vividly recall the words of my mother, "Who have

raw meat, seek fire." This phrase translates to simply means if you have something to get done it is your responsibility to get it done. So I listened to the words of my mother and made the choice to take immediate action by responding to the email. In the email I explained my background and financial situation, I did not leave any stone unturned. After two weeks of waiting for a response. I received a call from a lady who represented the selection committee for the scholarship; she told me that they have received my email and they cannot afford me the scholarship, because the recipient of the scholarship has already been announced and contacted. However, they have checked and allocated some monies to grant me a sponsorship instead of the scholarship. She then said I should report to the sponsorship office immediately, to follow through with collecting the sponsorship.

I shared this story with you so it may inspire you, to make the choice to never give up, whenever you are faced with rejection or opposition. But instead, make the choice to seek fire to the meat you have at hand.

9 MAKING THE CHOICE FOR BUSINESS

Today is April 16, 2018. This marks exactly 2 months since I made the choice to write this book you are now reading. At this exact moment, I am 33,000 feet in the air, traveling at 500 miles per hour; on a plane looking outside the window. The thought came to me that I have not done my daily writing. This thought immediately moved me to make the choice to start writing instead of just sightseeing at the clouds and ocean.

What I am about to write about in this section is not for everyone. This section is for those who inspire to be their own boss (business owner). But if you feel like reading along regardless, I will encourage you to follow through with your choice.

Businesses Opportunities Are Everywhere

As I sat on the plane while heading back home, the thought of "Business Opportunities Are Everywhere" came to me.

If for some reason you disagree with that thought, I suggest that you exercise some patience and continue to read along, as it will soon come clear to you.

Apart from writing this book to inspire you. In my daily dealings with others, I tend to engage in various conversations with people to stretch their minds, to start making the choices for their better future. Whenever I raised the topic of starting their own business, I tend to get various excuses. One being, they are no opportunities where they are presently. If you share the same sentiments, let me be in your face and say, you are wrong, opportunities are everywhere and I'll even go further and say, opportunities are endless. You just need to make the choice to train your eyes to see these opportunities.

Training Yourself to See Opportunities

Whatever you are doing at this moment. I want you to make the choice at this time to stop and follow along with this exercise, as I Illustrate that business opportunities are indeed everywhere. I want you to look around and locate a bottle of juice or a bottle of water from a distribution company. I am giving you permission to stop reading and go locate that bottle and place it to stand on its base. Do not be lazy. Stop reading and go do it now.

Now, I want you to pause and really take a good look at the bottle. You will see obviously the content in the bottle of course; you will see bottle itself; you will see label; you will see the cap; you will see the seal; on the cap, you will see a print of the company brand.
Now let us take any piece of the above-mentioned component and examine it. Take for example the label, I can guarantee that someone at some time or another, saw the opportunity and made the choice to developed a printing label business. If you keep looking at the label,

you will see the company's logo on it. That logo was designed by someone, who made the choice to develop a logo designing business. The material to make the label also came from someone, who made the choice to develop making materials to print on. Even the surface that the bottle is standing on, was created from a choice that someone decided to go in the business of creating furniture or whatever the surface the bottle is standing on. In case you missed it, the point I wish to bring across to you is simply this. In your busy schedule of life, I want you to make the choice to take some time to look at how many business opportunities exist around you - then make the choice to take action and any of those opportunities you wish. In case you still have a challenge in finding an opportunity, the following section on Network Marketing will help.

The Business That Change My Life

I can write to the moon and back for the rest of my life on this business concept, but I'll resist the temptation and keep it as short as is possible. Please do not hold me accountable on this, because I know I am going to go overboard. But this is a choice, I am willing to make because I know it will be of great help to you - *only if you are ready.*

Before receiving the proper education on this concept, like most people when not educated in a subject area. I was skeptical - outright I shunned it. But I am so happy I made the choice to give it a listening ear and a seeing eye nonetheless. In case you are waiting in patience for me to reveal this business concept, then here you go. The Business concept that change my life is what is termed as **Network Marketing**.

What is Network Marketing

What is Network Marketing you ask? Well, let me answer it this way. You have been doing network marketing practically all of your life, without being compensated for it. Let me illustrate. Have you ever told anyone about your favorite book, Fifty Shades of Grey or about this book that you are reading; Or how about your favorite movie; your favorite store; your favorite restaurant, your barber, your hairdresser, or even your iPhone? Unless you live in a world from the movie, "The Gods Must Be Crazy", then you most definitely have. Let me go a bit further in case none of the above applies to you. How did you heard about Facebook, WhatsApp, Instagram, Snapchat or any other social media platform that you currently use? Somewhere in your answer, you will say a friend, family member or colleague. Right? So Network Marketing is simple you recommending to people things that you like and love. When I really grasped this definition, that was when it started to make sense to me.

My Introduction To Network Marketing

At around 7:30 am, Monday, November 17, 2014, I received a message from my twin brother and it went something like this: "Biggy (By the way that is my pet name), Biggy we going to be rich, we going to travel the world. Just watch the video below." Please note this was not the way he should have introduced it to me. The video was about 13 minutes long and in my mind, I did not have the time to watch it, plus I was getting ready for work. So I told him that I would watch it when I get to work. At about 10 am, he messaged me to asked if I had watched it. I told I will watch it on my lunch break. At 1 pm he texted me again, this time I told him I will soon look at it. This went on for a week, so to have him stop annoying me about watching that video. I reluctantly made the choice to watch it. My mindset at that time was anti-network marketing, so I stop about halfway into the video and told him that I watched it. He then asked, if I was ready to be a part of the company and I told him no. I came up with all kind of excuses, from having no time to having no money to do this business. I, however, told him, that I would help him by sharing the video with other people.

Fear of Loss

In keeping with my promise to help my brother with this business, I made the choice to invite a few of my friends to a seminar that they were having about the business opportunity. To my surprise, a few of the invitees were excited about what they saw and decided that they wanted to start the business. If these persons were to get started before me, it meant that I would not earn any commissions for my efforts. This fear reluctantly forced me to make the choice to get started. I wish I could say getting started was a smooth process, but it was not. I wanted to get started, but I could not come up with the money – at least that was what I thought.

No Money Excuse

After making the decision in my mind that I was going to get started. My mind politely asked: "how are you going to do that?", "are you forgetting that you are broke?" As those thoughts came into my head, I could recall the presenter during the presentation stating that " many of you are seeking financial freedom and this is a vehicle that has proven all across the world to provide just that. But your minds are going to be your biggest distraction from making the choice to gain financial freedom."
With that recollection, I went to him and told him that I wanted to get started, but I cannot find the money to do

so.

He looked at me, smile and then ask. "So you're telling me that I am supposed to believe, that you cannot locate 365 USD, to do a business that will provide you with financial freedom?" I looked at him squared in the eyes and replied, "Unfortunately, I cannot locate that money."

He then asked me, "How many days are in a year?" I answered confidently, 365 days.

Great, he proclaimed and continued to say: "If you see this business opportunity right at this moment and you cannot come up with only 365 USD, it means you have not saved at least 1 USD a day. You have not saved a bottle of soda or beer money per day. This only means whatever you have been doing for the past year or for your entire life is not working for you.

You need this business, more than you think it needs you."

I was quite upset and angry. This man was insulting my ego; however, I made the choice to remain humble and listened. In continuing he said, "I can understand that you believe you cannot locate the money, but that's not true. Because people long before you have found a way to locate the money and people long after you will do the same.

Some people borrowed loans, others asked for assistance from friends and family members, yet a few sold their personal belongings, people have done all sort of things to come up with the money. So if you really want to get this done. You will drop the excuse, because it is an excuse, and let us find a way to get you started.

I am glad that he spoke to me, the way he did; because that talk opened my eyes to see that I could indeed borrow the money. The next day, I made the choice to borrow the money, and because of that choice; you are now reading this book to receive inspiration to go after your dreams and goals. Make the choice to drop the excuse of not having the money and find a way to come up with the money to make your dreams and goals a reality.

The Microwave Syndrome

You read it correctly, yes the microwave syndrome. In the world that we live in today, everything is moving so fast due to the advancement in technology. So people have become so caught up in getting things right now, instead of being patient.

You place your food in the microwave and literally within minutes it's ready. However please be warned when it comes on to business or any other worthwhile goals, it will take some time to reap the rewards. You just need to make the choice to be patient and continue to do, the daily disciplines that are necessary for building your business.

I find it that most people grossly **overestimate**, what will happen in one day and grossly **underestimate** what will happen in a year. This is due to the microwave syndrome that we have been exposed to.

For the record, nothing is wrong with wanting to achieve your goals and dreams quickly. In fact, I want you to achieve them in the fastest time possible. But I have to be real with you so that you will have an understanding of the process, that is involved in accomplishing your business goals.

Along the way to accomplishing your business goals or any goals for that matter, you will realize that you are actually working your ass off for yourself. But I want to tell you, please take my advice and make the choice to not quit. But instead, make the choice to stay focus. And I promise you if you do this long enough, your dreams will definitely become a reality.

Going back to the statement, of people **often grossly overestimate what can happen in a day and grossly underestimate what can happen in a year**. The best story that explains this is the story of the Chinese Bamboo Tree.

This tree obviously grows in China. But what is shocking is that this bamboo tree takes 5 years before it bore the earth surface after the seed is planted. What is even more shocking is the fact that, this seed has to be watered every single day for 5 years. If for some reason during those five years, the farmer forgets to water it. He has to start over the process again and water for another five years. As crazy as it seems when this process of watering this seed is complete. In less than 2 weeks the bamboo shoots up, fully grown to provide a wonderful view.

I share this story with you, so you will make the choice to be patient and focus on the bigger picture, of what you are working to achieve. Make the Choice to be patient and again, believe me, you won't regret it.

Business Education

Network Marketing, is arguably the only place to get real-life business education. I went to school for about 20 years of my life, I even did a subject in high school entitled, Principles Of Business. However, the education I got during my 20 years in school, cannot come close to the education I have received, by making the choice of getting involved in the industry of network marketing.
Making that choice, as not only afforded me be to travel; to increase my income; to increase my mindset; finally becoming an author. But this choice turned me into becoming a business owner of a media company.

The business education or the overall education that I have received is amazing. Many times, I sit and wonder where would I be, or what my life would be like, if I had not made the choice to get involved in the industry of network marketing.

In this industry, you get the chance to associate with very successful individuals, from authors to motivational speakers. I believe it is these associations that cause my life to turn for the better.

It is said that you will become like the people you associate with. So stop at this moment and look around your circle. Are your friends going places, do they have the drive to win, do they encourage you, do they want you to be successful. If you can't say yes to any of these questions, then you need to find a new set of friends.

Please don't misunderstand what I'm saying. I am not saying to get rid of your friends. But If you really want to achieve your dreams and goals, you need to have limited association with those who are not encouraging your success.

When was the last time you read an entire book from cover to cover? If you're like most people, I am guessing you cannot recall. Right?
The reason for you not recalling is that a study was done on how many books a person will read after completing college and it revealed, the answer to be **Only ONE(1)**.
That is no big deal until you add the facts, that in this fast-paced world that we are living, the old way of doing business is changing rapidly. So if a college graduate only will read only one book after graduation; what type of education do you believe they possess to keep up with the time?

I suggest you take my advice to make the choice in reading just 10 pages per day of a book, on a subject area in which you need to be educated on. By making this choice consistently for a year, you would have read at least a dozen books in the area you which to pursue. The average book carries about 300 pages. So can you imagine in one year; you will be much smarter, than the people who graduated at the top of their class in college. When I understand how powerful this was, I made it a mandatory choice to read 10 pages each day of a book in the area I choose to develop.

I am suggesting you make the choice also, in order to gain the education necessary for accomplishing your goals and dreams.

Objections to Network Marketing

Prior to writing this book, I have had over 3 years of experience in the industry of Network Marketing. These 3 years of experience have allowed me to gain so much understanding of how the human brain typically works, when presented with a networking marketing opportunity or an idea. 98 percent of the time after an opportunity is presented, there is always an objection as to why they don't believe they are not able to make use of the opportunity. These objections include but is not limited to the following: I Can't Find The Money, I Have No Time, I Am Not A Salesperson, I Have To Talk to My Spouse, It Is A Pyramid Scheme, I Have To Think About It. Has any of these objections reminded you of yourself, whenever an opportunity was presented to you?

Other than the objections of, It Is A Pyramid Scheme and I Have To Think About it; I believe that I have written lengths about the other objections in this book already. Nonetheless, let me make the choice to review them all because learning comes through repetition.

I Can't Find The Money

Has this statement ever been a response, you have used when presented with a networking marketing opportunity or any opportunity for that matter? Well If yes, then you are not alone. I too use to use those words as well. However, upon realizing that our brains have the power to provide the answer to everything we need. I made a choice to refrain from saying, I Cannot Find the money. Instead, I ask myself, how can I find the money. The choice to ask ourselves a question puts our mind in action to find solutions for solving the challenge that is at hand.

You not only can use this technique for financial reasons but for anything at all that you really need. Just ask the question of, **how can I?** And an answer or answers will be given to you. All that is left for you to do, is to make the choice to take actions on the solution.

So whenever again you feel like saying you can't afford something that you need, catch yourself and instead make the choice to ask yourself, **"How can I?"** - and just trust your mind to deliver, it always will.

I Have No Time

If I had more time on my hands, I could make use of this opportunity. Only if I had the time I could be a success. Statements like these are what I received from people as it relates to the objection of not having enough time, after they have looked at an opportunity. We live in a world where we get 24 hours a day. However, if you need more time, you simply have to wait until the strike of 12 midnight and look around for the extra time that was left over from the day. Please let me know if you are successful in finding any.

Please don't take that advice. If you do so, you would be diagnosed as a mad person. I was just kidding because the reality of life is that everyone has the exact amount of time. It is what we do with our time that makes the difference why someone is becoming a success and the other becoming a failure.

Our days are broken up into 3 sets of 8-hour blocks: simple Mathematics; that is a total of 24 hours. The first 8 hours is for sleeping, The second 8 hours is for school or work and the remaining 8 hours is supposed to be used to work on yourself in becoming a success.
Correction, you have 11 hours remaining to work on yourself. Because the average person sleeps only 5 hrs out of 8 hrs, so we have 3 hours unaccounted for. Hope you're following along with the simple Mathematics. So that 3 + 8 = 11 hours. Yes, I can hear many of you debating that you need way more sleep than that, because you work very hard - and I applaud you for working that hard. Also, you may still be debating that you have to work on the job for way more than 8 hours. Again, I hear you and I understand what you are saying. However, to settle your debate; I will just borrow this statement from my mentor, Jim Rhon. It says, "If you work hard on your, Job you will make a living. But if you work hard on yourself you will make a Fortune". This statement is so straightforward, I know you get it.

Many of us are guilty of not working hard on ourselves, but instead, we work hard on the job. The sad news, however, is that when the pay cheque arrives at the end of the week or month we become upset, of not getting the pay that we truly deserve. Then we go back to the job we dread to do, just to start over the never-ending circle of the rat race.

I am fully aware that, I have digressed a bit off the topic of not having enough time. However, I believe this digression, as at least causes you to stop for a while and assess your life situation.

Getting back to the time objection: all of us are left with 8 to 11 hours, to work on our self, in becoming the best we can be. However, most of us use that time for social media, gossiping, watching television, basically, we unconsciously watch those hours go to waste every day. Let me say this before you start crucifying me. Nothing's wrong with social media or television, because life should be a balance and we need to take a break at some time. However, when we spent too much time engaging in these activities, we are setting up our selves for failure. So the choice that I want you to make each day is to find something to do with those 8 - 11 hours that you have. So that your life would be exactly the way it was made to be.

I Am Not a Salesperson

A salesperson is, someone who is well-dressed, with a briefcase and documents in hand, knocking on doors and making calls to make sales right? Nope, sorry to burst your bubble, that is not the only criteria that define a salesperson.

A salesperson is anyone that is involved in selling. Let me say it again, a **salesperson is anyone that is involved in selling**; and the truth is, we are all salespeople. If you immediately objected to this statement then you sir or madam, you have just proved the point to you yourself. Your mind started or at least tried to convince you of the idea that you are not a salesperson - and that my friend is selling.

Selling is the highest paying profession in the world, no one can dispute that. We are all into sales, and let me prove it.

When you were younger, have you ever attempted to convince your parents on why you need a certain style of clothing or gadget? Or in your job letters and interviews did you try to convince your prospective employer on why you are best suited for the job? How about your spouse, did you attempt to convince them that you are the best fit for them? Or if you have children, have you ever try to negotiate with them on what to eat or at least to be quiet for some amount of time? Yes, I know you have, and all of that is selling. We all take part in selling every day.

Take a look at Oprah, Jay Z, Beyoncé, Lebron James, Usain Bolt. What do they all have in common apart from saying they are celebrities? Exactly, they are all salespeople just like you and I. All of the people that we celebrate on their success has some form of an endorsement deal with a company, which they advertise (**SELL**) for. You also do the same thing. What brand phone are you using: Apple, Samsung? What is the brand on the clothes you are now wearing? How about the car that you are driving? Or even the pen that you write with, what is the brand on it? They are all branded and you indirectly is being a brand ambassador (**SALESPERSON**) for these companies, without you even being aware.

I say all that to let you become aware of the unique ability that we were born with, the ability of selling. And now, I want you to make the choice to embrace this God-given ability and use it to make your dreams a reality.

I Have To Talk to My Spouse

The fact is, we will not always have the support of our significant others in all our pursuits. This is true even if accomplishing this goal will create a better life for you both. I believe this lack of support most times has to do with our partner trying to protect us from harm. However, please be mindful that our partner may not be the best person to give you advice on something that he/she is not qualified to give advice on. Please note: "**Only Take Advice From People Who Are Qualified to Give**

Advice." Your spouse may be qualified in preparing a Chinese dish or maybe qualified in fixing the plumbing around the house. However, he/she may not be the best person to give you advice on a business opportunity. So take my advice and make the choice to be careful who you are taking advice from.

Let us look at another fact. Have you ever had an awesome idea that you were so excited about and you rush and laid it all out to your partner, just to see them shoot it down? Not a great feeling, believe me. I have experienced this several times, only to my own regret. Please note I am not advocating making decisions without involving your partner. What I am advocating, however, is not to allow your partner or anyone else for that matter, cause you to experience a feeling of regret of not going after your dreams.

Let me share a quick story with you to end this section. I can recall sharing a business opportunity with a young lady; she was so excited. So excited that right after the presentation - she rushed to me and told me. "I am ready to get started to experience this lifestyle, I am just going to talk to my husband because he is overseas at the moment." My response was, "I totally support you consulting your spouse. However, if your spouse was to not be in agreement with what you have seen tonight, despite the obvious benefit to your family, would you still go ahead and join our business?" She responded and said, "Yes of course!" The next day, I called her and asked her if she was ready to get started. Her voice had lost all the excitement, she previously had the night prior. She said, "I do not believe I can go through with it. Long and short my husband is not in support of it."
I ran into her about 2 years after that call and asked how her family was doing. In no uncertain terms, she held down her head and point to her wedding finger, to show

the missing wedding band. She said, her husband decided that he no longer wished to be in a relationship with her, leaving her with bills up to her neck - which she has no idea of how she was going to clear it.

In the back of my mind, I started to think. What would her life be like if she had made the choice to make use of the opportunity that was presented to her 2 years before? I strongly believe if she made the choice to follow through with the decision to get started, even though I do not know what the future holds, she would have been in at least in a better position to handle her expenses.

In closing, I am suggesting you make the choice that is right for you, to avoid having a feeling of regret.

It Is A Pyramid Scheme

Do you know what are Pyramid Schemes? Are you sure, you do know what Pyramid Schemes are? I asked this question because so often after sharing a network marketing opportunity, I am hit with the statement, that it is a Pyramid Scheme. So let me try my best to shed some light, and hope that this light will enlighten you in really understanding that Network Marketing opportunities are not Pyramid Schemes. Firstly, pyramid schemes are illegal.

Have you ever taken a look at a hierarchical structure of an organization, whether it is a church, a bank, a small or big corporation? What is the shape of this structure?
If you say a triangle or pyramid, you are absolutely correct. Because every organization has a pyramid structure.
For example, look at a typical Church. At the top of the pyramid, you have the Pastor, then at the next level you have a few Evangelists, and at the level below this you have even more Missionaries, and at the foot of the pyramid is the rest of the church congregation.

Let us take the bank also as another example. At top of the pyramid, you have the CEO, then below that position, you have a few Managers, below the Managers comes the Supervisors and below Supervisors, you will have a bunch of Tellers and Customers Service Reps. That is a Pyramid, right? I do not believe you need to do a course in Business to understand this structure.

To be completely honest with you, I can understand your misunderstanding of believing that Network Marketing Companies are pyramid schemes. This is probably due to the fact in explaining the compensation plan (i.e. how commissions are paid to representatives in a network marketing company), a pyramid structure is frequently used. This illustration, if not properly explained may appear that the people or representatives that are at the top of the structure make monies off the people at the bottom. And if that was your answer, when I asked you earlier what is a Pyramid Scheme, then your answer is partly correct. People who are at the top of the structure do get paid from those that are at the bottom. Also, those same people who are at the top do assist those at the bottom to get paid. As a matter of fact, anyone at the bottom of the pyramid can and most often out-earn and outrank the people at the top. This phenomenon is not the case with any other organizations.

At no point in time, can the teller in a bank out earn the Manager, not even if that teller was to do all the overtime that is allotted to them.

So after all that, finally to the big question. What is a pyramid scheme? A Pyramid Scheme is the exchange of money, where there are no goods or service offered. As a member of a Network Marketing Company, a Representative will pay for a membership and this membership will provide them with some product(s) or some access to a service(s), for them to use or for sale to other people. This type of operation puts Network Marketing out of being classified as a Pyramid Scheme. At this time I hope that I have provided you with enough information to clarify your misunderstanding. So the next time you are presented with a Network Marketing Opportunity, you will be in a position to make an informed choice.

I Have To Think About It

Are you a parent? If you are not, I want you to pretend to be one just for a few minutes; so I may be able to illustrate a point. If you were to receive a call saying that one of your children, the one who is most well behaved, is stuck in an elevator, which is on fire in the city. Would you stop to think about it? Or would you make the choice to do whatever is necessary for rescuing your pride and joy? The answer is so obvious; you would without a doubt do the latter.

So the question is, why would you say you need to think about it - when you are offered a network marketing opportunity to create the lifestyle that you need?

Let me answer by saying. We make the choice to stop and think about things instead of making the choice to take action, simply because we do not see it as high priority or at least that is what we tell ourselves, that it is not of major priority at the present moment. In other words, the **Why Power** is not present.

Seeking information about an opportunity that was presented to you, is totally different than saying, I will think about it because the FAT truth is most times - we do not put any thinking whatsoever after we say we will think about it. Here are some facts that back up this statement. A research was done and they discovered that after 24 hours the mind will forget 75% of what was presented and

at 36 hours it will forget 90% of what was presented.
So basically, saying that you have to think about it, is you making the choice to fail. What I propose you do, however, is if and when an opportunity is presented to you. I want you to make the choice to refrain from saying that I have to think about it. Because you and I know, you really not going to get back to it and if you eventually do for some miraculous reason, you will only recall 10 % of the of the information, which is not enough for you to make an informed decision. Instead, I want you to make the choice to seek more Information, whenever you are presented with an opportunity - so you will be able to make an informed decision.

And this is the end of my not so long story, on Network Marketing. I hope this has created a better viewpoint for you, on this industry.

10 MAKING THE CHOICE FOR HEALTH

It is so ironic, that as I reach the topic on health; I received some not so good news. I received the news from my doctor, that I am diagnosed with Leukemia. I was like, "What is that, a fever?" He looked at me with a straight face and said: "no, it is cancer of the bone." I responded by saying, " Oh! It's just cancer, what do I need to do to get rid of it?" Again, he looked at me with a straight face and said, "Omanzo, I wish I could say this in another way, but this is serious. You can be treated however, you have a severe case, because of the choices you have neglect to take for your health. I am surprised you are still alive."

I put on a nervous smile on my face, to try and hide the shock of the news. Then he said, "it is ok, what I want you to do, is try to enjoy life as much as possible." He gave me a referral and said, I should contact him if needs be. I ask what he meant by enjoying life. He replied and said, "Omanzo, you have a terminal illness so the best thing you can do is enjoy life as much as possible."

If you were to receive news like this from your doctor, how would you respond? How would you take it? Thank God, that the above story that you just read has no truth whatsoever to it.

OMANZO BARRETT

Nonetheless, I shared this fictitious story with you, to carry your mind to a place, for you to become conscious of the health choices that you need to make daily. Life can be shortened, if we do not make the correct choices that are beneficial to our health. At this time I am going to dive into a few habits that we often neglect to take control of. I hope after reading this section, you will be moved to start making the correct choices for your health.

There are many choices we need to make, in order to create a healthy lifestyle. However at this time, I will just keep it simple and go with these Four (4) Choices, namely: the Choice to Exercise, the Choice of Food, the Choice to not Smoke and the Choice to Control Drinking.

The Choice To Exercise

Be honest with me, when was the last time you exercise? If for some reason you are thinking that you exercise every day, because you run to catch the train, bus or cab every day; just perish that thought. It is good if you run to catch transportation each day, but that in itself is not enough to be considered proper exercise.
If you answered and said, today or any day in the past 7 days; I applaud you. Keep up the great work and continue making the choice to exercise.
However, if you are like the majority, your answer will not be anywhere close to a week, maybe not even a month, for it was so long you have no idea when last you actually exercise. Maybe it was when donkey was a boy.

Exercising is really important for our health, there is absolutely no doubt about that. Unfortunately, many of us do not make the choice to exercise. I cannot say to you that I exercise everyday but whenever I see myself or I should say when colleagues start to take notice, that I'm out of shape and actually say, "Omanzo you are getting

102

Fat! (thank God for their honesty)." I immediately make the choice to get back to my exercise routine.

You might be thinking and saying I would love to exercise; But I can't afford to go to the gym, but I don't have access to a park to run, but I don't have the time, but, but, but…. But nothing! Do you want to be in shape, do you want to be fit, do you want to be here for a long time to see your children children's? Of course, you do.

So I am saying to you, just make the choice and drop the buts. All that the buts do is give you permission to accept your excuses and remember your excuses doesn't produce results.

I was in that place of finding excuses just as you, to not exercise; nevertheless, what I did to counteract these excuses; was to go online to locate different work out videos that I could do from home. Making that choice, eliminate me going to the gym which means, I could work out any time of the day that was convenient for me(morning, noon or night.)

The beauty about these videos is that they are free because I got them from YouTube.

So if you are really serious about your health and fitness, as I believe you are, I suggest you do the same.

"Can I be honest with you?" I guess I can; after all, you have made the choice listen to me throughout this book.

I **Hate** to exercise. Yes, I said it, I do not enjoy working out at all. It is no fun to me whatsoever. I literally have to drag myself every time to work out.

Nonetheless, I get it done regardless because if I neglect to exercise and keep fit, I indirectly make the choice to develop an unhealthy lifestyle.

So if you are like me and you dread to start that exercise, that you kept saying that you are going to start. Make the choice to pull yourself and just start. Even though, I dread to start the workout; whenever it is completed I get energized. So just make the correct choice for your health.

The Choice of Food

It is said that you are what you eat. I disagree because I love to eat; ackee and saltfish (Jamaican National Fruit - or is it? Not the place to have this discussion); I love to eat eggs (fried or boiled); I love to eat ice cream (cookie and cream, grape nut, rum and raisin flavors). Hmmm Hmm Hmm. Can you actually taste the ice cream flavors? Well, I know I just did.

Even though I love to eat these foods, I am neither an egg nor an ackee neither am I an ice cream.
I am just kidding; we are really what we eat, but not to be taken in the literal sense.

I am not a health nutritionist or do I claim to be one. But most times we as individuals, are aware of certain foods that are bad for our health and yet still, we make the choice to succumb to those urges.

Let me share an example with you. My fiancé has a major issue with the consumption of dairy products; it causes her face to break out. However, she loves her milkshake with strawberries from Burger King. So from time to time, sometimes too often, she will make the choice to go against her better judgment and indulge her sweet tooth. Literally within minutes, she would start to break out with pimples.

Yeah, yeah, I know this is a very simple story. But I share it with you for you to ask yourself the question. Are the foods that I am about to consume good for my health? Is it really what I should be consuming? If the answer is no, then simply make the choice to just refrain from it. Even though the urge can be really strong, the choice ultimately lies with you.

The Choice to Not Smoke

At the age of 14, I succumbed to peer pressure and made the choice to indulge in smoking marijuana. Yes, it was indeed a choice, whether I was pressured by my peers or not, I was the one that ultimately made the choice. In case you are not aware, marijuana is an illegal drug and to make matters worse, I was not an adult. What was embarrassing was the fact that I was convinced that smoking marijuana would make me a brilliant student, a dumb thought I must admit. So with this thought in my head, I indulge almost every day in smoking. I didn't discontinue the habit until I got enrolled in college. At that time, I was 18 years old.

I was always fully aware of the bad that was associated with smoking. But it was not until I listened to a Doctor, who was giving us an educational talk during college orientation that smoking is bad for our health; before I made the choice to rid the habit.

The Doctor spoke on so many topics in his presentation: from hygiene to how many hours were needed for rest. However, what caught my attention is when he showed us two pictures on the presentation slide. One picture was of someone's lungs who does not smoke and the other of a person's lungs who does smoke. Just looking at the latter picture, it scared me. He went on to explain that all type of smoke is bad for our health: whether it be from an open fire, fumes from a factory or motor vehicle, second-hand smoking, or from deliberately inhaling the smoke.

This presentation motivated me to start making the right choice for my health. So I made the choice to indulge less and less in smoking each day, until today at this very moment; I can now say it has been way over 10 years that I have last smoked.

Whenever I see people, especially females indulging in smoking I always ask them the question. "Why do you smoke?" As a matter of fact, let me outline a conversation that I had with a young lady. On my way to the beach, I saw this young lady, smoking right in front of her 2 years old daughter. The conversation went like this:

Me: Why do you smoke?
Young girl: I don't know
Me: Are you aware, that smoking is bad for your health?
Young girl: Yeah, I am aware. But we are all going to die one day right?

I smiled, shook my head and walked away. Thinking to myself, "why would someone see a speeding car or a bullet and walk right into it?" Then the answer came to me, "It is her choice to make, whether it's to her detriment or not."

Now let me ask you a quick question. Have you ever taken a look at a cigarette package? What does it say about smoking and your health? It always goes something like this, "The Chief Medical Officer warns that smoking is bad for your health".

The weird thing about this warning is that, it is the boldness writing on the box, it is even bigger than the cigarette manufacturer name. Yet still, so many of us make the choice to not yield to the warning. Why is that though? Is it that we love the feeling it gives us? Is it that we do it because everyone is doing? Or is it that we get so addicted to it, that we cannot do without it?

To be honest with you, I have no idea what people really indulge in something that is clearly not good for their health: to each his own. However, if you have a machine that is producing gold, wouldn't you ensure you take the best care of it? Of course, you would. You would take the best care of it. Well, my friend, I want to inform you that you do have a gold machine and that gold machine is you. Just as you would take the best care of your gold machine it is the same way you need to take care of your health.

I am now suggesting if you are someone who indulges in the habit of smoking. I need you to make the choice to take the necessary steps or seek the necessary help to rid this habit because your health depends on it.

The Choice To Control Drinking.

Wine is a mocker, strong drink is raging, and whosoever is deceived thereby is not wise. Proverbs 20:1. I believe this is worth repeating. Wine is a mocker, strong drink is raging: and whosoever is deceived thereby is not wise. But what does this means though? I don't believe it is that hard to understand. It is a simple warning against the habit of indulging in strong drink (alcohol) because it is simply not a wise choice for your health. If you grasp this point, then you do not have to read any further. However knowing the person you are, I know you are going to continue.

Have you ever witnessed someone who had a bit too much alcohol in their system? It was embarrassing, right? And it hath to be so. How about you, have you ever gotten to that point of drunkenness: not a good sight at all. Or how about hearing your friends and family members or even business associate going over your behavior from a previous night.
For those who have indulged in alcohol and have not reach the point of drunkenness. I can hear you loud and clear, "that will never happen to me because I only drink occasionally." So quick question, do you believe that every single person, that has gotten drunk, deliberately decided or planned to get drunk? Of course not, it most often starts with just an occasional drink.

Please note, I am not saying that you should not take a break and chill sometime. However, they are many ways to chill other than indulging in alcohol. Furthermore, it is proven that the drinking habit can lead to many health issues, major health issues at that.

Take a quick read of this analogy. If your car uses gasoline, would you drive up to the gas station and order diesel? I doubt you would. Likewise, your body does not operate on alcohol so filling it with same, would eventually lead to a breakdown.

I used to indulge in the habit of drinking at least 5 times during the week. My favorite drink was Campari. I always had a bottle in the house; this was a part of my monthly shopping list. Wow!! Just thinking about it, made me realize what a stupid choice I used to make. Whenever I went to play pool, which was every evening after work I would indulge in my favorite drink. Did it improve my game? Nope, it absolutely did not. Why did I do it? I guess the fact that when you are in an environment with others indulging in a habit, it is just easy to follow their lead. Most times, however, if we are not careful, following their lead only leads you astray.

In the next chapter on Making The Choice For Relationship, I will share how important it is to ensure you choose the right environment to be apart.

In bringing a close to this section, I believe that it is fair to say that we all want to live as long as is possible. However one of the key factors that will determine this, as to do with how we treat our body. So again, I am suggesting you make the choice to break whatever bad habits that you may possess that is not conducive to your health. The choice is yours.

THE CHOICE – STEP INTO THE LIGHT

Sometimes Others Need To Make the Choice for Your Health or Vice Versa

Despite the above heading being extremely long, it holds a lot of truth. So please continue to read along to receive the truth it holds.

At this very moment of writing these lines, I share the living room and kitchen area of an apartment with a couple. Let 's refer to them as Roy and Pam. They have a daughter that is 5 months old at the time of this writing. Pam had decided that she had gained too much weight after giving birth to their daughter, so she made the choice to get back in shape.

One day, while I was sitting around the dining table, writing this book of course; Roy quietly walked across the living room in the kitchen. He then reach up to the cupboard, took out a pressure cooker, open it and pulled from it a black bag. In this bag was a box of frosted corn flakes. So I enquired, why do you go through all that trouble to hide the corn flakes? He told me that, "Pam wanted to lose weight. However, she constantly indulging in these food items, that is contrary to her losing weight. So I have made the choice to hide the corn flakes from her."

Other than seeing Pam and Roy story as just being plain funny, I want you to take the time to get the lessons as well.

If we are honest with ourselves often times we may not be as motivated, inspired or have the courage to make the correct choice for our health. As a matter of fact, we may not have the courage, to make the correct choices for anything worth achieving. So it is not only important, but it is also necessary that we appreciate the choices that others have done for us, or impressed upon us in going after our goals. Likewise, it is necessary that we always strive to assist others in making the correct choice in achieving their goals as well.

At this time, I want you to take a register of all your family members, friends, colleagues, and associates then ask yourself; what choice can I impress upon them to assist them in achieving their goals. (Stop reading now and make the choice, to see how you can be of any assistance). It can be something as simple as making a call to share a kind word to keep on trying, or better yet, you can have them get their hands on this book that you are reading or any other material that will inspire them in becoming their best self.

I know you're going to do it because that is just the great person you are. So keep making the correct choices and continue to help others do the same.

11 MAKING THE CHOICE FOR RELATIONSHIP

Taking a glance at the heading of this chapter, you may be thinking that this chapter is about choosing the correct spouse. If that was your was thought, then you are partly right because I will shed some light on that in the latter of this chapter. But for now, I want you to understand that relationships do not only happened between spouses. They happen between parents and children, between business associates, between teachers and students, relationships are between friends as well.

Have you ever heard this statement before, "birds of a feather flock together"? How about this one, "show me your friends and I will tell you who you are"? These statements were told to me constantly by my mother, whenever I went out of line. I could never get too much of these warnings. Even though I heard these statements over and over, it didn't become clear to me until age 26 at a seminar in Florida. At the seminar, the speaker was explaining the laws of association, and mention these two other statements, "**You are the average of the 5 people you spend your time with**", and "**If you hang around Losers, You will become a Loser**". As I sat there writing those statements in my notes, it hit me between the eyes like a bullet. This was what my mother was trying to say to me all those years.

What made it even clearer was when the speaker said: "**If you have 4 broke friends then, you are the 5th.**" Ouch!!! This caused me to start considering all the relationship that I was a part of, that wasn't in line with me accomplishing my dreams.

Let me use an example to illustrate how the wrong choice of friends can lead you to failure, and then share another example to show you how the correct choice of friends can lead you to success.

Let us say that you have 4 close friends, and your goal is to receive first-class honors in the degree you are pursuing. This means you have to make the choice to spend more time in completing assignments right? Now, let's say your four close friends, who are also in college, they prefer to hang out instead of doing assignments. So every night they will come to you, asking for you to take a break from your studies - so you all can go relax at a club and have some fun. For the first week or so you have managed to withstand the pressure. But by week 3, the constant pressure of them coming to you every night; telling you how great last night was and where they are heading tonight and of course, they want you to come with them. What do you believe your choice will eventually be if they decided to keep prodding you? The answer is so obvious, you will most likely take up their offer. Accepting this offer would be the choice; you inadvertently make to kiss your hopes of achieving your goal of a 1st class honors Truss (Goodbye in German).

On the flip side, say you have 4 close friends who have made the choice that they will be graduating from college with first class honors degrees. You, on the other hand, is just in college to just get enough to pass by, and you love hanging out more than spending time on your assignments. Do you believe these 4 friends of yours will make the choice to follow your lifestyle? Or would they remain steadfast to their goals, forcing you to eventually start adapting to their lifestyles of spending time on your assignment? Well, I think you know the answer.

So at this time, I want you to take a deep look at yourself and ask the question. Are the friends that I am associating with, are they motivating me, are they inspiring me to go after my dreams and goals? If for some reason they are not, you have the choice to find other friends. After all, it's your goals and dreams and not theirs.

How Do We Associate?

Before we go into explaining how we associate, let me address a challenge I believe you might be having in disassociating from a longtime friend, colleague or family member. Trust me I know it is hard to just suddenly get up and look a someone you have known for years and say, " Hey Mike or hey Michelle, I have known you for years but this is where I draw the line because you are not motivating or inspiring me to go for my dreams and goals." If that was what you had in mind, I suggest you perish that thought. What I want you to understand, and start practicing is what I call **Limited Association**. This is self-explanatory. It simply means, you limit the time that you spend with certain individuals. Please note, not every individual are worthy to get our time. I know it sounds harsh, but it is the truth. I am sure you know at least one person who is so negative, that they will start developing in a dark room. (One of Les Brown jokes).

These people, do not only see the glass as half empty, they will go as far as to look on the rainbow, and tell you that the colors are wrongly arranged - now that is sad. These individuals should have limited association in your life. That is if you are truly serious about accomplishing your dreams and goals.

113

Answering now the question, on how we associate. We associate with others in so many ways than we understand. We associate in person, we associate through the radio, we associate through the television, we associate through social media, we associate through the books we read. As a matter of you making the choice to read this book is you indirectly making the choice to associate with me. You may not know me, however through reading this book you have developed and created a picture of who I am. I do hope however that this is a good picture, a picture that is inspiring you to make the correct choice for your dreams and goals.

Apart from all the ways that I have mentioned above, on how we associate, I also want to spend some time explaining the importance of associating through inspirational books, audio tapes, and videos. We all need some inspiration at some time or another.

So making the choice to read an inspirational book, listening to an audio tape or watching a motivational video is you associating with the creator of that content. The creator had you in mind when he was putting the content together.

Let me say it another way, I had you in mind; Yes, YOU, reading these words right at this moment. I had you in mind when I made the choice to write this book. I know that I cannot be in person beside you each day to inspire you to make the correct choices in creating your best life. However, in this book I am right there with you: on your bedside table, in the dining room, in your bathroom, at school or even on the beach, wherever you decided to take me - I am there to inspire you. Even after I have left this world, my message of making the right choices will still be here with you, to inspire you. Isn't that magical? You are able to associate with me as you read. So at this time, you may be looking for inspiration from a mentor but for some reason, he/she may be so far away, for you to get in direct contact. However, what I want you to do though, is to stretch yourself and make the choice to get your hands on any content that this mentor has produced. Through this or these contents, you will definitely be associating with them.

Surround Yourself With The Thinking That Out Thinks You

What does this mean, surround yourself around the thinking that out think you? Before I go into explaining, let me share how I got this quote. In October 2017, I attended a seminar entitled, Millionaire Mindset. The key speaker was a guy by the name of Johnny Wimbrey. This guy is a phenomenal speaker. He's an entrepreneur, an author, a speaker as I said before and of course my mentor (He does not know he is, but he mentors me through the contents that he produces, from his talks and though his books).

I was sitting in the seminar when he said, " in order to be successful you need to surround yourself around the thinking that out thinks you." Then he repeated it again for emphasis so that the audience would get it., " **In order for you to be successful, you need to surround yourself around the thinking that out thinks you.**" To be honest, I didn't get it right away, and maybe you too also do not get it. So let me explain. As humans, we make a huge blunder and tend to have more of a negative mindset instead of a positive one. We even make a greater blunder, to believe that we know everything. But the reality is that **we don't know, what we don't know, about what we don't know**. (If that statement confused you, make the choice to keep rereading it until you get it)

To get an understanding of a specific subject area, it is

necessary, that we surround ourselves with people that have the knowledge on that subject area. In other words, it is important that we associate with these individuals thinking.

For example, say that your goal is to become a medical doctor. I am not a mind reader, even though at times I would like to believe that I am. Anyway, as you think about becoming a doctor, you may start to believe it's going to take too long, it's going to cost too much, I am too old to venture in that field, I am not qualified to be in that field. With this kind of thinking, you absolutely will not achieve that goal. However, if you were to be surrounded by some doctors, or associated with some doctors, the thoughts of becoming a doctor wouldn't be so far-fetched. By being around their thinking, you would be motivated and inspired to know that you have what it takes to a become doctor.

What you might have missed, is me making the choice to be at that seminar in October 2017, to receive this message; was me surrounding myself around the thinking that out thinks me. I was receiving valuable information that was needed for me to make the choices that are necessary to achieve success. What you might also miss as well is you making the choice to read this book or any inspirational book for that matter, is that you are making the choice to surround yourself around the thinking that out thinks you. You're actually getting the authors thoughts in a book form.

I hope that this was not only informative, but it will also inspire you to make a deliberate choice to surround yourself around the thinking that out think you, whether through a book, a video, a seminar and even in direct contact: your success depends on it.

Harmony

Today is April 8, 2017, at this very moment I am sitting on the floor in my fiancé's room writing this for you. If you are reading these lines now, then it means she is no longer my fiancé, because I have made the choice to call off our engagement. (At least that was where my mind was at).

One of the key factors in any relationship, whether it be business, marriage or friendship. There must exist a spirit of **HARMONY**. In case you missed it, the word Harmony is written in all caps and bold to show the importance of it in any form of relationships. As I write these words I am sitting and looking at my fiancé in bed. Apart of my mind is convinced, that I am booking a flight to return back to Jamaica, 9 days earlier than planned. While the other part of my mind is saying, stick it out. Keep reading to see how this story unfolds.

A fork in the Road

My fiancé is a fun, loving, very animated person. As a matter of fact, let me use her favorite word she is super animated. I first laid eyes on her while I was covering an event on a beach in Jamaica for her mother. This was almost 2 years ago, to this present day of writing.

How can I forget, she was wearing a bright yellow dress, which was lit by the bonfire that was on the beach. This added more flare to the moment. As I approach her to take her picture, I discovered she was a bit shy. I also noticed that she was friends with another girl I knew quite well. This girl turned out to be a blessing; she was the one that convinced her to let me have her contact number.

After she returned home, I reach out to her and we had simple conversations - just to get to know her. From time to time, I would encourage her about school, and how she should pursue her passion. However, in about 6 months or so, our communications seem to no longer exist.

A Real Life Fairytale Story

Almost a year after we met, her mom reached out to me and requested my service to cover her 50th birthday celebration, at the Trident Castle in Jamaica. Little did I know what was about to be unfolded. She arrived late at the birthday celebration, just as her mom was about to cut her cake, due to an airline issue. After cutting the cake with her mom and 2 other siblings, I beckoned to her that I need individual pictures of her. We starting conversing and she explained, why she arrived at her mother's birthday celebration late. She told me that the airline had left all her stuff in New York; leaving her with nothing to wear because all her clothing, that she carried to attend the weekend of upcoming events, was in her luggage. As usual, I told her not to sweat it. Something will work out, it always does work out for the best.

After capturing her pictures, I went back to finish up the work that I was contracted to do for her mom. Upon completion of my work, I packed up the equipment, requested a drink and went to reside in a quiet area in the castle. And there she was in her blue dress, sitting in the dark. I went to sit beside her and was conversing again.

Please note, these lines that you are about to read below is no Fairytale. It was exactly what unfolded. She was holding a glass of drink in her hand and said to me, I love your lips. I smiled and said thank you. With a smile on her face, she said can I kiss them. I was a bit confused, I thought that what she was drinking must have had an influence on her wanting to kiss me. However, we went ahead and kissed. At that point, it was not anything magical. Not until she said, "this is my first kiss in a castle and WOW it is also our first kiss as well. What are the odds of this happening in this day and age and who's going to believe us when we tell them." Hearing those words from her was nothing less than magical. I was experiencing what I called a **real fairytale**. After our magical kiss, she went back to the bar to get another drink, as well as to inquire what was in her drink. To my surprise, there was no alcohol in the drink. So there was no outside influence on our first magical kiss in a castle.

Opening Myself Again for Love

Let me start by saying I Omanzo Dwayne Barrett, is no saint as it relates to females. This should not be interpreted as being cocky or anything of the sort. I am just sharing this with you, so you may understand where I am coming from. I am what many will consider to be, Christian Grey, from Fifty Shades Of Grey. As a matter fact I was often called that by various people. (I actually had to catch myself and make the choice to write various people instead of various submissive). Again this is not something I am proud of ok.

Before I continue, let me take you back in time; to when I closed myself from love. On February 14, 2010, I did my first wedding engagement. Very easy day to remember, it was Valentine's Day. And she said Yes!!! However, 3 months later she said No. Her exact words were, "I love you Omanzo, but I am not in love with you. I am in love with someone else." Even to this day whenever we talk, I always joke with her about this statement. This is some 8 years ago to the present writing of this book, enough time to get over my heartbreak.

Did I regret that it happened? Back then in the moment, of course, I regretted it. But now I have no regrets. If that had not happened I wouldn't have met my fiancé. I would have no reason to be on that train in New York City to be inspired to write this book; as a matter of fact, there would be no way possible you could be reading this at this moment.

After that heartbreak, I shut my heart away from love. To be honest with you when I hear people use the word love, I use to question if they really meant what they were saying. So for 8 years. I forced myself to not give anyone access to that part of me, and then December 14, 2017, it happened. At 5 PM, I got the call that our mother is no longer with us. She passed at the age at 60, at that point in time I was just 4 days from turning 30 years old. This prompt me to look at my life and assess myself; if I am blessed enough to live to see the number of years that my mother lived, then it means I have the next half of my life to live. So I made the choice to not allow the next 30 years of my life to be like the last 30 years. I made the choice to refrain from engaging in my promiscuous lifestyle. This decision was long time coming, but when my mother past I literally took a 180 degree turn. Not many people were happy with my choice, but I had to make that choice to open myself for love again.

December 27, 2017

On the above date, I was on the phone with my Joshanna; we spoke for hours and hours. I listened to her entire life story. Many of the struggles she underwent as a child as well as all her dreams and goals. My heart went out to her and I was shocked to know that she had experienced so many struggles, behind that smile of hers. After I came off this long conversation, I called my twin brother and told him I think that I am going to give my love to her. He was shocked, after all - he knows every single thing about me. He is the only person who can continue on with my life, if

I was to pass away - just to show how much he knows me.

I followed up with my decision to open up myself for love again, by contacting her Aunt as well as her friend. (The friend that was on the beach, when I first met Joshanna.) I told them of my intentions to ask her to be my wife in Florida, because we had planned to travel there in January 2018, and I needed their assistance in getting her ring size. I not only made the choice that I wanted to spend the rest of my life with her. I also make the choice to go online and picked out the perfect ring, that would match her style. However, due to the time I was traveling out of Jamaica to Florida, the ring would not reach to Jamaica on time. So my brother and I travel literally travel across the island of Jamaica to find the perfect fit.

A Twist In The Story.

Continuing the story on the topic of harmony, from the beginning of this chapter; I am now making the choice to be very vulnerable to you, so you can get a better understanding of where I was at. As I was there sitting on the floor writing away, my fiance called a friend of hers and deliberately put her phone on open call, so I could hear the conversation. This conversation was nothing nice to hear. All I could hear was the criticism. I was laughed at, jeered, call all sort of names; to say the least. "How can someone who said they loved me and said yes to be my wife, really be doing this?" This was just one of the question that came to my mind. It hurt me to my core, and at that point, our engagement was done. Our forever after was over.

Fight or Flight

Let me define what this means before I continue with the story. Fight or Flight means, the instinctive physiological response to a threatening situation, which causes one either to make the choice to resist forcibly or to run away.

After hearing that insulting conversation, I did not hesitate with my choice. I went directly into flight mode. I made the choice to book the first flight that I could get on that was heading to Jamaica. As I was looking into flights, Joshanna started to beckoned my attention. But I was upset, hurt and furious. I am the kind of guy that whenever I am upset I will not utter a word - I am a dead mute. I knew that the silence bothered her a lot; but at that point, I really did not care. She kept asking me, what are you doing on your computer? And I continued to remain as silent as a lamb - looking into flights. She started to throw the pillows at me, then she came to the floor and close down the laptop screen. I then got up and told her that I needed to go home. I needed to get back to Jamaica as soon as possible. She literally got up, turned around and step through the room door. Then in about 15 seconds, she returned. She threw her arms around me and said, "please Omanzo don't go." I was still furious and upset and didn't want to hear anything at all from her. She asked me to lay with her and I did. However, in my mind, I had already made the decision, that as soon as she leaves for work I'll be on the first flight back home. I was exhausted from the early morning flight that I took to be there with her, plus spending majority of the night at her Aunt 60th birthday celebration; so I fell asleep. Upon arising, I honestly had no idea what happened, except that; I wasn't feeling that upset anymore and the feeling or taking that flight had gone.
So I make the choice to fight for our relationship, instead of taking flight over something that was as trivial as not wanting to be on the dance floor at her Aunt 60th Birthday celebration.

Let me make it clear, I am no relationship expert, neither

do I aspire to be one. All I request of you is to take the lessons that I share in my story and make the choice to fight for your relationships; instead of making trivial matters damage or cause ruin to your relationship with your spouse, or anyone else for that matter.

CLOSING WORDS

Throughout the entire reading of this book, I spoke extensively about choices and how important they are in leading you to success or failure. So at this moment, I am going to share my penultimate story with you.

Your Choices Have Serious Consequences

Today is May 6, 2018, which marks one of the worst days of my life. I had to listen to my fiancé calling me all kind of names: you are germs, whore, evil, liar - just to give you a few examples.

And she was 100 % right to use all those words; I deserved every last one.

As I said before this is my fiancé and I have made a stupid choice, to cheat on our relationship. It happened multiple times which was downright unforgivable. A choice I wish I could take back, but I could not. I lied to her face and promised her that I would never engage in any more promiscuous relations. However, I have betrayed her trust.

Prior to the above date mentioned we were great, happy and in a healthy relationship. We had plans, we had hopes, we had dreams of creating a legacy for our family. But on that dreadful day, I was being compensated for my wrong choices.

On Saturday, May 5, 2018, I was reading a book entitled; "The Power of the Positive Mind", by Norman Vincent

Peale. In chapter 3, "How to Have Constant Energy" he shared a story about a businessman who was having an affair with a married woman. He became guilty and decided to break off the relationship. However, the woman threatened him that if he chose to do so, she will enlighten her husband concerning their escapades. The businessman became aware that if she was to do such a thing, it would affect the high moral standing that the citizens in his community had of him. So he decided to not go ahead with his decision. But the guilt and fear kept on bothering him to where he could not get to sleep.

Long and short of this story he when to speak with Mr. Peale. Mr. Peale then advised him that he should break off the relationship and assured him that whatever he did that was right would turn out right. **ONE NEVER DOES WRONG BY DOING RIGHT**. He urged him to just do the right thing and **Put the MATTER in GODS HANDS**. He did what he was told, and the women acted by her better nature and released him of the guilt.

Upon reading that story, It had an impact on me. I needed to come clean with my fiancé, and do what was right. So I decided to let her be aware, of my wrongdoings and to leave the matter in God's hands. I was also prepared, to deal with all the repercussions that were going to come because of my wrong choices. If she decided against continuing our relationship, then so be it. I have done her wrong and if that is my consequence, then I have no choice but to accept it. So please as you're reading the last lines in this book I want you to look at your life and make the choice to not place yourself in a situation such as this. If for some reason you are in a similar situation, I am suggesting you make the choice to do the right thing and come clean. In doing so, you remove the heavy burden of guilt and fear, so you can place your full energy into making your dreams a reality. By not doing so, you just may as well destroy your dreams.

You have now reached the end of this chapter and also the end of this book. My hope for you is that something in this book as not only touched you. But something in these pages has inspired you, to make the choice to do whatever is necessary in making you become your best self - that you were destined to be. As we part, let me say thank you again for making the choice to read, "**The Choice: Step Into The Light**". I really appreciate it. Now please make the choice to not only reread it. But also make the choice to pass it on to others, so they too can make the choice to be inspired in becoming the best version of themselves.

The Choice Is Now Yours.

Made in the USA
Las Vegas, NV
18 July 2021